Volume One

Growing Up Psychic

On Ghosts and Visions

By Kathryn Anne Ellis

2007 Kate Ellis
Revised 2020

ISBN 978-0-985483-6-5
TXu 1-603-060

The Healing Quest Publishing
Scottsdale, Arizona

Contact information: kellis19@hotmail.com
Website: www.thehealingquest.com

Facebook: Kate Ellis

Facebook.com/thehealingquest

Facebook.com/psychic.clairvoyant.medium

Acknowledgements

My thanks to Robert Romano who encouraged me to put fingers to keyboard and share my story and his dear friend Hannah Goldstein who counseled me legally, and hours of encouraging talks and emails along the process of writing this memoir. Thanks to Kay McNeary who created the front cover design from my suggestion from fond memories of enjoying the "Highlights" children's magazine which has a feature of 'find the hidden items' in a picture. They are still publishing to this day. Thanks to Lace Jaze who completed the back cover design and gave me the leaves design running throughout the book. To Melissa Pritchard, Author and faculty at ASU who told me when she first received the manuscript she had just run a hot bath, and brought it with her and couldn't put the book down, sitting in a freezing cold bath, until she turned the last page. Melissa advised me to find a great editor for refinement but not change my voice. Many thanks to the Bergen County Historical Society of New Jersey with research assistance, and "The Record" newspaper for archive assistance and photocopies. Thank you Google, you allowed me to find information without leaving my seat. And my greatest thanks to my editor, Juliette Paradise. Her dedication and meticulous pencil, keen attention to details made my head swim with corrections on every page and practically every paragraph. I was on the verge of allowing this volume to be published posthumously. As any good friend, she lied to me and said the minor changes would take tops, twenty minutes. It is three months and twenty minutes later.

Please note that I did not use all suggestions made by my editor. This volume is written as I speak. I politely ask all English majors and purist of the American/English language forgive some of the grammatical license so generously taken.

Contents

Chapters

Prelude

People say to me; “I wish I could do what you do...” and trace off looking into some undisclosed fantasy-land.

...If they only knew my journey.

Introduction

What a strange, strange trip it has been! I do not recall being born, but I remember choosing my parents. I cannot immediately tell if you intend me harm or joys, but I can see your life clairvoyantly by the simple posing of a question to me, and give you information that crosses the boundaries of time and space. I haven't correctly aligned the numbers of the lottery, yet I can solve great mysteries...

Life is a strange, wondrous place. I understand it as much as you... Sometimes, sometimes a little more. Sometimes I find great comfort in Richard Bach's book "Illusions: Adventures of a reluctant messiah", or the Dhammaprada, sayings of Buddha, and then there are so many years I am lost, just confounded! Sometimes I wish I could 'see' my answers. Is it truly the pursuit, the challenge of attaining? I'll let you know when I remember.

This is the first of three volumes that present the trials, tribulations and triumphs of a life being a clairvoyant medium. I choose not to change a thing.

Kate Ellis

"Growing Up Psychic"

Chapter One

The Old Man on the Toilet

Have you ever wished to give back to a parent? Had a desire to 'gift' them something big, perhaps something they never had before, or to give back to them after a life of trials and hardships? Most kids want to provide a big luxurious house with all the modern amenities, a place, where there are no survival concerns or worries. To design a paradise that is nurturing and supportive, as we once were as children. My Mother, Yvonne kept a roof over our heads and loved us. This moment finally arrived for lavishing my personal dreams and aspirations for my Mom, a place without worry or concerns of survival or comfort.

I was happily married with a toddler and a house, I began to prepare a space, a nurturing home in the finished basement of our home hoping Mother would accept an offer to allow myself and my husband Daniel to support all of her worldly needs in Chicago. We intended to offer her a private space all her own in the finished basement that had a half-bath, a living-room area, office space, and bedroom. I'd began to have these very vivid dreams of my Mother being on a small boat alone on the ocean, no land in sight and a storm approaching. This dream persisted for many months. I thought that the dream perhaps related to her being in Arizona without her family? My thinking was that she could come back to Chicago and live with my little family, and pursue a college degree and become who she always wanted to be, had there been time raising three children, and working (at times) three jobs to support us. We were all now grown, my older brother Bruce, younger sister Karen and I, all off on our own journeys in the great wide world, carving out lives for ourselves. I pondered the question; "how could she refuse?" I discussed the idea with my husband Daniel, which he readily supported!

Daniel and my Mother had always got along very well. He enjoyed her hugs and pecks on the cheek. His family wasn't particularly demonstrative of affection. By contrast, Mom would reach out and grab Dan as he walked by, warmly kissing him on the cheek and holding him in a bear-hug, until he embraced her back. He would act as though he just put up with it, but secretly appreciated the attention.

Dan and I planned that Mom would have her own private apartment. Dan told me he thought it was a great idea, understanding and appreciating the financial struggles she had endured, now raising his own family, and he was comfortable with the plan.

Before presenting the idea to Mother, we slowly made the basement apartment homey. I sought out my good friend Jill, who had talents in near anything one needed to know especially on a domestic level, including upholstery! Years earlier she helped me re-make an old camelback Victorian-era mohair couch from old blue jeans I had collected over the years in our last apartment. Jill jovially agreed to assist with the interior design of the basement apartment; she adored Yvonne, having been a mother-figure as well as a friend.

When my husband and I bought our first house, the previous owners had left behind some matching furniture pieces: a small love-seat and chair with an ottoman. The furniture was downright ugly! It was very worn and covered in a brown and tan plaid pattern. The pieces were simply utilitarian, not a pretty sight in the least.

Over the phone Jill and I had made a date to go shopping for the tools and fabrics we needed, and met a few days later. After much searching in fabric shops around the city with not much luck, Jill suggested we go to the Rag Factory. It was a six story free standing red brick warehouse in my old neighborhood, and had probably been there since the Columbian Exposition. Inside the building everything was thick with dust from all the fabrics and plasters dust, although it seemed asbestos was the more likely culprit. You could see the air through sunlight streaming in through the windows. Searching for the right fabrics was a day-long excursion, not unlike a treasure hunt. Jill and I waded through thousands of feet of warehouse per floor, scurrying up and down the old, well worn wooden stairs that creaked with each step, and bowed in the middle. Some of the rooms had deep bins full of items you had to rifle through; other areas were organized with reams of fabrics on ten foot high shelves. Eventually, I found a heavy duty fabric in a cheery bright red, (mom's favorite color) with a floral overlay, and more polyester batting than one would use to create a king-sized quilt! We spent the entire afternoon traipsing through every inch of the warehouse, and eventually left with everything we needed for the project. Onward to a well deserved cup of coffee at our favorite greasy-spoon restaurant, Bob's Egg Palace.

Jill and I re-upholstered and re-shaped the furniture pieces into an overstuffed, luxurious and comfy sofa to rest after a long day. We softened all the harsh straight edges of the couch, easy chair and ottoman, glue gun and sewing needles in hand. My husband contributed his carpentry talents and created a storage space within the frame of the loveseat with fragrant cedar wood. It all slowly, in a few months, came together. I purchased a feminine daybed with white scrolling metal and brass, and covered it with a white eyelet comforter with new hot pink sheets (her second favorite color). We divided the basement well; Yvonne had several micro areas of an apartment while my husband, an amateur ichthyologist, still had room for several tanks of cichlids and critters and a desk.

My husband Dan's hobby eventually began to take over our small bungalow home. At one point, I was living with over twenty-two fish tanks on the main level! sense of the constant sound of the motors of the filters running 24/7 made me feel like I was living under water, the non-stop noise of the air bubbles breaking the surface the tanks constantly were personally taxing to my harmony! Now, we all have idiosyncrasies; I discovered I have 2 ½... I cannot stand the sound of running water, flute music, and driving behind vans. Its 2½ because I am working on the van issue... I did very well dealing with the sound of the bubbling water, for the most part, but eventually I had to put my foot down and asked Dan to please set up his tanks in the basement. I had suggested it could be his very own private getaway, being I only went to the basement to do laundry. This idea definitely appealed to him and so, over the course of a few months all but two tanks remained on the main living level. Dan had used one of the 35 gallon tanks set upon a nice maple cabinet to create a partition, essentially dividing the basement into two sections, essentially creating two personal sanctuaries for both himself and Mother.

After a few months, the preparations were completed. The basement really came out well. It was a comfortable, well planned space with all the creature comforts one needed.

I had had another dream of Mother on a small boat upon the ocean. This one was different from the rest in that now, there were colors in the sky as opposed to the drab gray and dark storm clouds moving fast from all directions towards her. Hues of pale reds, and orange with flickering gold's glimmered in the distance along the horizon. The storm clouds still lingered threateningly, yet as I observed her looking towards the light, a sense of relief embraced her as though cloaked by a warm blanket, and as she focused upon the dancing light, the boat began to move in the direction of the expansive horizon.

The next day I decided to place that phone call and present my idea to my Mother; beforehand I went out and bought a pound of espresso roast coffee, planning on a long conversation. I brewed a strong pot and call Mom at her home in Arizona, knowing it was her day off, to ask her if she'd consider our offer. This conversation would need to be handled delicately, yet without room for refusal.

My Mother Yvonne had always presented herself as a strong, self-sufficient woman. With that kind of independence, of autonomy, one develops a certain pride within, which is great for self-esteem, but can be detrimental in accepting assistance or help from others. I was very concerned that she might be gracious and thank us for the offer, but decline.

After brewing a potent pot of coffee, I dialed the phone. Mom picked up after a few rings, pleased to hear from me. I asked her to please listen uninterrupted. Noting the tone of my voice, she agreed. I carefully chose my words as I prepared a presentation of my family's desire to give her the opportunity and gift of a lifetime, time; time to change her path and fortunes in life. To create a life she always desired. I aimed to reassure

Mom that my family was in a place of financial stability, and we would have more than enough room for her. I told her how Dan and I, even her granddaughter, Jr. and Jill created a mother-in-law apartment that was ready for her to move into, today... Mom quietly listened as I made my case. I wrapped the proposal up asking her to please consider coming back to Illinois; just store your stuff, and pursue your dreams for your life, one of which being of earning a registered nursing degree... "Find a new you, begin college and become your hearts' desire, actualize your potential! Become your vision!" I implored.

This became a long and intense pitch. Mom was truly surprised with this offer, for her, out of the blue, and how long we collaboratively worked to make her comfortable. I gave her all the reasons she is welcomed and deserves nurturing. Having her only grandchild, the girl she wanted didn't hurt the offer! Mom, I said, "you would be surrounded by family and love and support, and no financial worries..."
Once reassuring Mom through her many questions, to my great delight, she said, "yes", without a moment of hesitation!

Mother absolutely loved the Southwest and its two seasons, spring and Hell. But, the economy was not strong in the late 1980's in Arizona, and jobs were becoming few and far between. Mom worked as a caregiver for the elderly, being a certified nursing assistant, a very labor intensive job that demands all of your attention and sometimes your emotion as well. It has all the rewards of knowing you are making a difference in somebody's life on the most intimate levels, however, the pay does not reflect all the energy demanded. While I secretly remodeled the basement; she was wondering as the scheduling from her multiple nursing registries's dwindled, what she was going to do? Even though we spoke frequently, I was unaware of how difficult things had become for her financially. At the time of our offer, she had less than a grand in her bank account.

Mom began moving preparation by acquiring a storage unit and gave notice to her nursing registries, as I planned to fly out and pick her up. It was late spring of 1989 when I arrived in Phoenix. I felt like I was home, back in the Southwest.

Near ten years ago, my Mother, Sister Karen and I had moved to Phoenix in 1980. I never did want to move back to Chicago, but the recession in Arizona was so difficult in the early 1980's, after more than six months of unemployment, and literally collecting aluminum cans in the desert for cash, there were no alternatives left but to return to the Mid-west, to the two-flat Mom inherited from her mother, Susan. Mother had a friend Steve, a trusted friend overseeing the renting out and maintenance of the property. However, we lost contact with him while out in Arizona. No one back in Chicago knew where he had disappeared to, and the income from that eventually dried up too. We found out through other friends and sources that Steve had pocketed the rent money for a few months and had taken off! The worst of it, though, was that the property had not being taken care of. The two apartments were empty except for the kids and gangs using it as a hang out.

It seemed circumstances required us back in Chicago. Returning to Illinois around 1982, we walked into the house after a couple years being gone, finding that, anything that was not bolted down had been stolen! Both floors were totally trashed. The two flat was built in the 1920's. Three generations of my maternal family lived there: My Great Grandmother Victoria; Grandma Susan, and then my Mother Yvonne, and her family. The house had been kept in pristine condition. Unlike other homes in the area, our house was free of bugs and roaches, and no mice or rats, which has always been a difficult thing to achieve in the city. Everything in the apartments was destroyed or missing. Parts of the drop-ceiling lay in piles on the floor, the thermostats on the walls were torn out; the screen doors etc were all gone. What a mess! There was gang graffiti spray painted on the walls, and garbage piled deep and high on the floors through every room of both floors.

It is strange the way things work out. Opportunities were more plentiful in Chicago and the economy more robust. Finding steady work was a choice, not a wish or desire. Never the less, I went back kicking and screaming.

I have discovered through my travels that every city has a flavor; and as soon as you hit the city of Phoenix the smell of creosote brush, sage and orange blossoms fills your senses. The sky is perpetually crystalline remaining items in the apartment, rented a small trailer and loaded it up. We both looked forward to a mother/ daughter road trip. It had been a good few years since we had the blue, and in every direction are the mountains creating the valley of the sun. People say, "Hi" passing on the street as opposed to the guarded sideways glance, you would expect back East. People have settled in Arizona from all over the world; yet somehow, everyone melds into an attitude indicative of the area: People are at ease, unrushed, and displayed calmness in spirit.

In 1984 Mother returned to Arizona, I had gotten married always planning on moving back to the gracious desert.

Now returning to 1989, Mom met me at the airport.

After arriving at her home, I helped her pack the

opportunity to hang-out together, living 2019 miles apart. We had a wonderful, unhurried journey back to Chicago, stopping off in New Mexico, and revisiting old town Albuquerque, my favorite place, discovered the first time we had traveled west. We then cut up to Santa Fe, an artists' community we had always wanted to visit and in which we had planned to shop. It was late afternoon when we hit the road heading north, and it quickly became very dark except for a full moon barely rising on the tree filled horizon. It was a beautiful, mountain road with deep dips and sharp curves. The edge of the pavement at times just cut off and led to a deep ravine; at other spots the thick forest came right up to the edge of the black asphalt. There was not much room for mistakes! And I was driving Mother's 1971 Ambassador. It was what I called like driving a land yacht! I had my doubts it would make the 2000 mile journey, never mind the mountains. It was definitely an adventure traveling up to Santa Fe, but treacherous road without the familiar street lamps to illuminate the dark winding and very deserted highway was a negotiation all the way. It was late as we started on the highway, and we planned on staying the night. In the morning we intended on exploring every nook and cranny of the town. We were both excited that we decided to hangout in Santa Fe this time around.

On the two lane highway, it seemed like we were the only people on the road that night, no glare of headlights behind us, and just a few cars traveling down the mountain passing.

The atmosphere however felt as though it was thick with spirits, both within the car with us, urging me to be cautious through incessant, barely audible whispers, and those that came into awareness along the mountain path, along the sides of the road. There was a moment I seen psychically a group of 20-30 native Americans walking beside the road, except that they moved *through* many of the trees, where at other times they moved around. A native male, who appeared to be leading the others made eye contact with me; and I could sense him, telling me to stop. I slowed down, and just ahead were several herds of deer and I had to stop to avoid colliding with the bucks, who stood in the middle of the faded yellow double lines in the road staring. Its eyes glowed in the bright headlight reflecting a greenish-yellow glow, stark against the indigo night; 6-8 doe's and very young fawns at her heels migrated across the black-top highway led by other younger bucks, lopping into the woods beyond into complete dark. After all the deer were safely on the other side of the road, the large, full antlered bucks standing sentry, quickly disappeared. As we waited for the herd to cross, the group of single file natives passed by, the man who communicated to me nodding his head to me, continuing their trek.

Experiencing wildlife up close and personal was thrilling; Being reminded that, life isn't just a gray cement ground with cement buildings blocking out the gray-orange sky experienced in the city, "I had forgotten!" I thought, as my mind also winding along, with

its own internal curves and drop-off's. I said a silent prayer to the Native American Indian for guiding me. I didn't question the experience. Mother and I eventually arrived in Chicago after a few leisurely days on the road. As interstate 55 led us into the city, the air condensed into the smell of diesel fuel, dirt and the aroma of an area occupied by people for a millennia. The highway's merged into one another; I 55 into 90/94 leading us deeper and deeper into the city of Chicago, finally arriving home and a new life.

Everyone in my little family had ample time to get settled into new routines. Mom was absolutely delighted with her little apartment. She immediately began researching schools and the pre-requisites needed for a nursing degree, and then began her first semester... a full 12 credit course load that first Fall! It had been more than twenty years since she had enrolled in a school. She was 53 years old. I was and still am awed and inspired.

The months went quickly by as we all enjoyed the easy rhythm of being together, as a family. One early afternoon Mom and I, both free of obligations sat down at the kitchen table with a pot of coffee and a fresh pecan Danish ring I picked up at a local bakery, to chat and catch up on the week's events. We had gotten on the subject of contests; as a young girl I had won a record album from a local radio station asking for weird stories. I called, actually got though, and told them of Tony the Ghost, which won me a record album by The Orleans!

Proudly, I recalled how it was also my first story that had been published in Fate Magazine of the "Chamberlain Avenue Ghost", the same "Tony" story. To be published by my favorite magazine was like winning the lottery! I still have the Issue sent to me in the mail with a thank you note.

As the afternoon wore on and we shared more memories of Tony, I mentioned my earliest recollection of strange encounters, that of the old man having died in the upstairs bathroom on Maiden Lane in Little Ferry, NJ. Mother looked at me askance as I paused to pour more coffee for the both of us. We had nearly finished the pot, and had managed to polish off half of the pecan ring.

Her mind went completely blank saying, "I don't recall anyone passing away at our family home." Somewhat perplexed, I related my memories...

... I am not sure what age I am, perhaps 6ish. There was a party for Uncle Tracey at our family home. My younger sister Karen and cousins Bonnie, who's my older brother Bruce's age; Robin, and Tracy were there. We, the kids, had become bored at this adults' party and wanted to pull out a board game from the living-room closet. I had worked up the nerve to ask permission from Dad if we could get a game out. He usually said, "No", and as predicted, he didn't want to deal with the toy pieces all over the place during the party and told me instead to go check on a guest who had gone upstairs, but hadn't returned. Now, being horrifically shy, I was not comfortable tracking down an adult. However, saying 'no' to Father was not an option; he had a healthy temper of which one wisely stayed on the good side!

I grabbed Karen to go with me. My sister and I opened the door to the hallway stairs leading to the second floor. We began racing up the stairs, pulling and dragging each other down every few steps, goofing around. We argued at the top of the stairs about who would knock on the apartment door. We came to the agreement that I would knock on the outer door. Gently, not really wanting to be heard, I tapped my fist upon the door a few times, receiving no response. Pressing my ear to the door, Karen doing the same, we strained to hear if anyone moved about... Nothing but silence! Cautiously we opened the door. We then moved from room to room, which was actually a tiny apartment. We were about to leave when I noticed the one room we hadn't checked, the bathroom. The Bathroom! Not a door I was comfortable knocking on. It was most definitely her turn to knock, but she wouldn't have anything to do with it! I grimaced at her with all the disdain of which I was capable, then gathered all my nerve and knocked on the bathroom door...No response, I knocked again...Nothing. We stood there in front of that door for what seemed an eternity!

I Eventually grabbed the door knob and slowly opened the door enough to peek through the crack. A strong breeze blowing through the sheer green curtains first caught my attention; my eyes then followed the fluttering fabric down to the wide hem, finding the missing guest, the old man. He was gently slumped forward, still sitting on the toilet. The old man never stirred and was very quiet; there was no movement nor did he give any recognition of my presence. Scared and beguiled, I sent my sister downstairs to fetch Dad, and listened as she stumbled and stomped down the stairs hurriedly. I moved a bit closer to this strange and curious sight. I took a few slow, but very brave steps toward the old man, thinking it was an unusual place to fall asleep. Someone came up behind me as I drew near the old man... and that was where all memory ended.

Mom looked at me quizzically, scrunching her nose. She then looked off into the distance thinking hard, searching through her memory, and then asked me, "who was the old man?"
I told Mother I thought it was a neighbor two houses down. She said, "Nothing like that ever happened when you were a child, no one ever died at the house

when we were children." I insisted that the neighbor did come over for Uncle Tracey's party! Saying, "don't you recall? He lived alone having no family left and you and Dad were being good neighbors inviting the lonely man over."
Mom said, "We only had one party for Uncle Tracey, and that yes, it was a birthday party while she was pregnant with me..." Then an incident during that party came flooding back to her. Mom said, "We ran out of soda during the party and I insisted on driving to the store for supplies, a very seven months pregnant with me. Returning from the store I arrived home to fire engines and police and an ambulance in the driveway." Sometime during the party, a guest used the upstairs facilities and quietly passed away of a heart attack.

Mom said; "I can't figure out how you could have known" since she couldn't recall the incident ever being brought up.

I wondered however about the premonition, of my sister, and younger cousin. They had not been born; there was only Bruce about 5 years old. Cousins' Bonnie and Robin, who were then just a few months old.

Years later as an adult, I found that I had several pre-birth memories. What is most intriguing is how the mind subconsciously created a context, a story, which is as real a memory, of an experience to this day I am absolutely sure I lived.

The little red house on Maiden Lane was not haunted as far as I "knew", but there were objects in the house that were. In the following chapter, it is this next unsettling incident, one of several, that fueled my intense dislike of clowns, primarily pictures of representations of them.

Chapter Two

The Haunted Relief

It was cleaning day in the little red house on Maiden Lane. Mom went about dusting the shelving and artwork mounted on the wall over the couch. I watched as she carefully used a feather duster along the edges of the pieces. I had several unsetting experiences with the items, and wondered if she was disturbing them; the pictures.

There hung a picture of a red-headed hillbilly girl in pigtail braids I didn't particularly care for. I didn't trust it. She always seemed to stare at me. What freaked me out is on occasion she winked at me! On the same wall, there was also this small (6 or 8 inch) plaster relief of a clown smiling with red painted lips and high arched eyebrows. I told Mom it would make faces at me. She tried to explain that that could not happen; it was just a plaster clown. I was not convinced! It occurred too many times. I secretly hoped in my thoughts that while Mom dusted the relief, it would fall to the floor and break! She did knock it hard soon after I had that thought, but it simply swung on the nail. Staring at it I could have sworn that clown frowned meanly at her. She straightened it out, seemingly not to notice as she whistled her one achievable monotone note, listening to opera playing on the radio.

After finishing that task, Mom pulled out the vacuum cleaner and gave me a coloring book and box of crayons to keep me occupied. I was a toddler, perhaps near two years old. She scooped me in her arms and sat me on the living room floor in front of my book. As soon as she went into one of the bedrooms to clean, I got up, making sure I was very quiet and climbed up on the couch, intent on studying the clown to see if it was still frowning. After struggling up, being very small, I pulled myself up onto the high back of the couch, grabbing the fabric with my toes for leverage and crawling up beneath the relief. Just as I made it up, steadying myself, and looked at it, all of a sudden, the clowns face jumped off the wall, but the relief remained hanging on the wall; it's "ghost" leaped out scaring me half to death! I raced down the couch, bouncing onto the floor screaming heading toward Mom, the ghost following behind in the air just above me! It chased me all the way around the corner into the master bedroom where Mom continued to clean, not hearing me over the loud motor of the vacuum. The transparent ghostly head of the clown then whooshed past Mom, above her head, and out of the closed bedroom window!

I ran to Mom, grabbing onto her leg, excitedly telling her what had happened. She scooped me into her arms trying to comfort me. I was so scared and freaked out! She told me I imagined it and took me back to the living room to show me it was still smiling. It took her a while to coax me to look at it as I clung to her neck, still crying. When we got back into the living room and to the spot where the relief hung, she took a long look at it. It no longer smiled but grimaced... A cold draft passed by us at that moment. She swung around, feeling a presence as though someone stood lurking behind us, as a cold chill ran up my spine, and hers I sensed too. I was not releasing my death grip, I was still trembling! My Mom's reaction seemed to validate my experience. I had told her on many occasions that the thing made faces at me, and it frightened me. The plaster relief was gone the next day!

I seemed to be the only one bothered by the plaster clown, but the picture of the red-headed hillbilly girl in pigtails winked at other members of the family, I discovered years later. Her eyes would seem to follow your movements in such a way that one 'felt' she was staring at you. My grandmother Susan had painted the picture, and it was very well done so throwing it in the garbage, (I would have preferred and burning it on a pyre) was not an option. Eventually it was placed in a closet, face against the wall.

Chapter three

The Lion

I didn't know it at the time, but I have a spirit animal protector. I was about five years old. It was fall and a powerful nor-Easter, a storm coming in off of the Atlantic Ocean, roared over our town. Mom put us all to bed, my older brother Bruce in his own room across the hall, Karen and I on bunk beds in our shared bedroom. I enjoyed having the top bunk, being high in the air. Mom tucked us in and said to go to sleep; she would be leaving for work soon.

I couldn't fall asleep. The storm grew violent, thunder booming, rattling the windows every few seconds. Lightning burst across the sky with giant violet and white fingers of fire reaching right outside my bedroom window, getting closer. The lilac tree a few feet away whipped around violently, bending to and fro as the wind pushed and pushed.

I called out to Karen, but she was fast asleep. I buried my head under the covers, but couldn't resist peeking out, fearing the loud crashing thunder storm, but fascinated by the beautiful lightning. A growing, internal awareness began 'sensing' something; a presence, energetic and powerful, something not outside my window, but outside my bedroom door!

I felt like I was being watched. The hair on my arms and at the nape of my neck stood up, feeling as though I was being pricked by hundreds of needles. I tried again to wake Karen, as the sensed presence became stronger and stronger, almost visceral. Then, I heard something growl, deep and guttural, and then something scratching on the other side of the door! Again, I called to my sister, to please wake up!

I was all alone, watching the lightning crash in the sky, and now this 'something' was persistently scratching outside the door. I listened carefully, moving to the other side of the bed, facing a few feet away from the door, and thinking I was hearing things as I opened up all of my senses, listening. I then moved back to the far end of the bed and tried to go to sleep, to escape, pulling the covers up over my head creating a cocoon inside the layers of crisp sheets and feather-tick comforter. It was unmistakable, though; there was a foreign sound! Under the covers, in a cold sweat, a moment of bravery assailed me. I decided to get up and open the door to find out what was scratching and whispering growls. In a burst of energy I threw the covers back and swung my legs over the wooden rail of my top bunk. Just as I did this, a bolt of lightning struck the lilac tree outside the window. The tree began to burn, split nearly in half. Then the door latch clicked. I whipped my head around, my eyes wide open fixed on the door as it quietly swung open. I watched the darkened doorway as a lion's shadow slowly filled in, as though it faded into reality at the threshold, inside my bedroom! I screamed as all this occurred simultaneously. I stared transfixed at the lion, startled, but without a sense of being threatened. The lion looked up at me, then, slowly, it faded back into a shadow. I paused in mid-movement, frozen like a snapshot in place as I prepared to jump down from the top bunk as this all happened. After the lion disappeared, I was able to let go of my grasp of the railing, and began to move, landing with a thump to the floor and onto the bottom bunk with my sister in what seemed a single motion!

Minutes later Mom came home and I excitedly told her what happened when she peeked into our room, checking in on us. I still heard the scratching, and asked her to listen. She did, and hearing the sounds she became alarmed, and told me to wait in the bedroom. Mom and now Dad checked all over the house, attempting to locate the source of the noises. Eventually they found in the small upstairs apartment a mouse caught in a trap, right above my bedroom! They came back assuring me that everything was okay, and the noise wouldn't scare me anymore.

Everybody in the house was now awake, Mom made hot chocolate and I forgot for the moment about the lion in all the excitement. The driving rain doused the burning lilac tree, and it eventually recovered after a couple of seasons and attention. I watched that bedroom door for a long time after that night, waiting. I didn't feel frightened but fascinated with the solid sense of power and strength and curiosity, great curiosity of that lion.

...

Mom was a great story teller and imaginative. She told me about Santa Clause, the Easter Bunny and of fairies that would sit quietly on the window sill. As much as I tried and watched, I never could see the fairies. The things I saw she couldn't see, either.

An intriguing incident occurred many years later with the same animal spirit lion: I was 19 years old on a road trip, so deep in a rural county of Kentucky, that one needed to know a bootlegger to purchase alcohol...

...I had met up with a man named Jimmy in Chicago who offered to take me on a motorcycle rally in Louisville, KY. The circumstances of how we met were a scenario out of a nightmare.

I was driving to a job interview late one morning that seemed really promising. At a traffic light on Western Avenue and 63rd Street the lanes narrowed for construction. (Chicago is known for having two seasons: Winter and construction) Some dude wanted to cut ahead of me and was honking his horn trying to get my attention, as a thick group of cars waited for the stop light to change. The idiot wanting to cut in motioned to merge ahead of me; I shook my head 'no', not agreeing. I motioned behind me, observing in the rearview mirror that the car behind had saved room for the motorist to merge into the lane. Then I turned away and stared straight ahead, ignoring him. The light changed and the cars moved along through the intersection that widened back into two lanes. The motorist who wanted to merge ahead of me became psychotic!

As traffic thinned, he sped up and cut in front of my car dangerously, continuing to drive. There were two lanes in each direction. If I was in the left lane, he would drive nearly on my tailgate, then speed up to get around my car and cut in front of me again, with only a few feet between our vehicles! I even pulled over to let him go on, but he waited a block or so ahead in a bank parking lot, as I passed, he began the harassment all over again, each time cutting closer and closer in front of me. Confused, I wasn't sure if I was becoming pissed, although definitely irritated, or if I was scared for my life! As I continued to drive determined to make my way to the job interview, the cat and mouse game finally ended when, cutting closer and closer, our bumpers connected. He had pulled in front of me, keeping pace with my speed. I decided; this is it! I'm going to lose this clown and maneuvered to the left lane and floored the gas pedal. Just as I began to merge over, he slammed on his brakes. We both stopped, I'm now seriously pissed, ready to tear apart whoever was in that car taunting me! Of course, the congested traffic we were in dissipated. No one was around, now. Stopped in the middle of the road, the dude jumped out of his car, running towards me as I jumped out of my car, angry, he claimed to be a police officer. I believed nothing at this point, though I did question his hardware. He was dressed in street clothes and certainly not acting as a professional police officer! He pulled out a gun and pointed it at me, but I refused to acknowledge its presence, which somewhat disarmed this maniac. Again, he screamed angrily stating he was a police officer and ordered me to sub mit as he holstered his gun. I got right up to his face, knees shaking as I confronted him, a large man about 6'1" and maybe 215lb. I weighed 104lb and have always been petite. My size never daunted me, however; I have always felt like I am 7ft tall and built like a gorilla! I asked for his supervisor, demanding a governing party on the scene. Oh, I was enraged and ready to go to physical battle with this crazy, threatening person claiming to be a peace officer!

Observing most of this up the road, three people; Jimmy, Chuck and Lynn sat perched outside on this gorgeous summer day at the edge of their used car lot, watching traffic go by, drinking beers. They witnessed the strange maneuvers of me and the irate mad-man approaching them from down the street. Jimmy, Chuck and Lynn happened to observe the vehicular maneuvers from nearly a quarter mile away. Our confrontation occurred in front of their used dealership. Jimmy stepped forward and asked if I needed to make a phone call. I said, "Yes, please!" and was ushered inside the office to call the police supervisor, and to tell him to haul his ass out here!

Chuck and Lynn kept the dude at bay, stating he could not enter their property. The supervisor arrived after twenty or so minutes later, and Jimmy walked me outside and stood on the curb protectively. Upset, I told the supervisor what had occurred and how the other driver tried to kill me over not allowing him to merge at the light. The dude calmly explained that I was the aggressor, and wanted me arrested!

The trio tried to interject, stating that they watched as we drove up the street and claiming HE was the aggressor.

This fell on deaf ears, and found myself spun around and handcuffed by the supervisor! I wound up being arrested! The person in the other vehicle was in reality an off-duty police officer, and his story of me being the offending party was enough for the supervisor, despite the witnesses' testimony. As I was being loaded into the squad car, Jimmy offered to hold my car when they threatened to impound it and grabbed my keys.

Handcuffed and brought to the police station, I now found myself standing in front of a tall wooden and white marble counter, observing rows of desks just beyond with uniformed men in varying states of obesity, a box of doughnuts half eaten and the smell of burnt coffee, and about a hundred years of sweaty bodies gracing those precinct walls. I had no idea what was going on! I can't recall hearing anything. I certainly wasn't read my Miranda Rights. They did discuss whether or not to remove my cuffs as I was turned around and lead toward a holding cell somewhere around the corner. All of a sudden Jimmy was there, walking up the marble stairs as I was being lead to a holding cell, to post my bail! Then he took me out to breakfast and bought me about a dozen cups of coffee!

After that ordeal, Jimmy and I met up a few times as friends at his local watering hole, a biker bar I was unfamiliar with. A new dimension of the world cracked open, and I became skilled at the game of pool, Jimmy taught me the science and art of shooting pool. I wanted to keep in touch so I could pay him the $75.00 back; he said it was his pleasure to help me out of a bad situation.

One evening, a few months after we had originally met, we hooked up again at the biker bar. He at one point attempted to kiss me, which I refused. Jimmy mentioned before we parted for the evening of a motorcycle rally coming up soon. A long weekend getaway, and he asked if I would be interested in going? He said that Chuck and Lynn were also going, and that after the rally we were going to Chucks Grandmothers' house out in the countryside to cut the lawn and have a barbeque. I told him I would think about it. A week later we met again for our now regular pool game and Jack Daniels get together. Jimmy again brought up the rally in Kentucky, and asked if I had made a decision as he walked me to my car. As we sat chatting in the car, I told him that if I accompanied him, it would have to be platonic. He said, "Yes, of course, not a problem!" I wish I knew at the time he didn't know what the word 'platonic' meant.

I hadn't a clue what a motorcycle rally was about, but discovering that people from all over the country drive and gather for a weekend long party, which sounded good to me, this could be a great vacation! The morning we left, eight to ten bikers met up right after dawn to travel as a group to Louisville, KY. The morning was crisp, but clear. I climbed up behind jimmy onto his Harley motorcycle and held on to the sides of his thick leather jacket, and off we went. As we neared the Indiana border, the sky grew heavy with dark gray-black-burnt orange clouds. We could see lightning ahead and heard a deep rumbling of thunder above, and feel it rise from the pavement beneath us. The group gathered under a viaduct to discuss the situation. The decision appeared to be made for us as sheets of rain opened from the sky. It rained so hard that it ran parallel, in sheets to the road sideways. We couldn't drive faster than 15-20 miles an hour, as we were pummeled by the cold downburst. Not fun! Totally drenched, we found a motel off the interstate, and we all checked in, Chuck and Lynn sharing the room with us. We shivered while waiting our respective turns for a hot shower, chilled to the bone by the storm.

Perhaps the storm was an omen, a warning, begging me to turn around and go home.

As we hung out waiting for the violent storm to pass, Chuck and Lynn went to fetch food for all of us at a restaurant next to the motel. Alone and relaxed, Jimmy again made an amorous move towards me. Surprised, I reminded him of our agreement. He appeared puzzled, but backed off. An unpleasant feeling lodged in the pit of my stomach, and again the thought arose that maybe I ought to simply turn back, catch a bus back to Chicago; However, Chuck and Lynn returned with the food shortly after, and I forgot my ruminations. The storm lasted the entire day and night. So we stayed the night, without incident, and continued our journey at daybreak. We arrived at the rally in Louisville in the late afternoon. There was row after row of bikers- leather clad men and women, drinks in their hands, vendors of all sorts, and an atmosphere of fun. Everyone was in high spirits as I followed Jimmy, who was reconnecting with pals from out of state and talking to others who recounted being caught in the storm in Indiana. I started to become comfortable with this eclectic group of people who, underneath all the metal and leather, tattoos and weather worn faces, were actually normal folks! I did not realize there was any danger around, but as my luck would follow, I found it.

As I began to feel secure and confident, I decided to take off on my own, exploring everything going on. I met a couple of guys, had a great conversation and was offered to join them to smoke some pot. I agreed. I found Jimmy in the crowd and said to him, "I am going to hang out with those guy's", pointing them out, and said, "I will catch up with you later." He said, "Absolutely not!" Jimmy said, "You cannot go off with those guys," forbidding me! I thought this was completely ludicrous, and turned around to go about my way...He grabbed my arm spinning me around and looked me square in the eyes and said, "It's not a good idea," changing his tone, where I detected a note of serious concern, and danger. Jimmy said, "I promised to keep you safe, and you need to listen to me." I paused; something inside strongly felt that he was right. So I stowed my bruised ego and did what he said. I stuck close to him. Later, we found out that a girl had gone missing from the gathering. The police were actually called and they found her not too far away, dead in the back of a van, and had last been seen with the three guys I had met earlier. I have maintained for a long time that I am not a lucky woman, but I am a blessed woman!

After the rally ended in Louisville, we went to Chucks Grandmother's farm. After settling in, Jimmy planned on taking a trip out to the bootlegger, and asked everyone what they wanted. Of course, being a dedicated Jack Daniels connoisseur, I elected for a bottle of green label. Jimmy shook his head quickly from side to side saying, "I can't drink that shit, it makes me crazy! He asked me to promise him that I wouldn't allow him to drink any Jack, and that I'd make him stick to his beer, and I agreed. He returned after a couple of hours, bought the liquor from the bootlegger, and proceeded to get drunk from a second bottle of Jack, that he stashed and sipped without my knowledge, as the beautiful summer afternoon of barbequing, hanging out and snipe hunting lingered into the evening. Yes, I went snipe hunting!

With twilight, the yard sparkled with fireflies, and the air was filled with the sounds of croaking frogs and birdsong coming from the woods just beyond the freshly mowed grass. The trees created a border between civilization and the wilds.

When it came time to retire, Chuck and Lynn already had the master bedroom. I asked Jimmy, "what about our sleeping arrangements, who would score the couch and who drew the second bedroom?" He said, "You can take the bedroom." I said, "I will be fine on the couch." (Jimmy was a big man, near 6'2" and at least 260-300lbs) Jimmy said, "I won't be sleeping on the couch, I will be sleeping in the bedroom with you!" "Yea, no, this is not acceptable," I said. I was informed I had no choice. I tried to get the attention of Chuck and Lynn and began banging on their bedroom door, yelling for them to please come out and help me. I was ignored, as I heard them making love on the other side of the door. I decided it was time to leave. I would rather be wandering out on a country road, groping my way in the dark than, being given such an ultimatum: Sleep with him or sleep with him. I was repulsed and feeling betrayed! I left Chuck and Lynn's door and peered around the corner to see where Jimmy was. I didn't see him and marched to the front door, grabbed the doorknob and then, Jimmy came up behind me with a large kitchen knife in his hand! I somewhat froze, looking him dead in the eye, defiantly. He then grabbed a hold of my wrist and attempted to put the knife in my hand saying, "If you don't sleep with me, you will have to kill me." I couldn't believe what I was hearing, confused. I said, "You are crazy, I will do no such thing." He twisted my hand until he placed the long knife in my hand with the blade pointed towards his belly, and thrust himself against me! I gasped, the scream lodged in my throat. I fell back from his weight, landing on my butt and he splayed on the floor in front of me. The knife had fallen to the floor, and a scrambled rush of him and me going for it. I reached it first and threw it across the room, got up and headed for the front door. He fumbled around, retrieved it before I could turn the doorknob, and another struggle ensued. He again grabbed my hand and thrust the knife in my palm and screamed, "Kill me, kill me now!"

I threw the knife further, and it landed behind a television set. I thought this time I would give myself a little more time to escape. No such luck, he found it again. This occurred a few more times until I gathered my wits and headed to Chuck and Lynn's bedroom and began pounding on the door, begging them to please come out and help me! Lynn yelled back at me finally, telling me to go away! I said, "He is trying to kill me, please come out for a minute and calm him down." No one came. I lost track of Jimmy. I decided to go for the front door again. I reached it, turned the handle and then I felt something cold and hard against the back of my head. It was a gun. Jimmy said, "You take one more step and it will be the last one you ever take." I froze, time slowed as though it had stopped. I closed the door reluctantly, frightened. As I stepped away from the door, turning towards him, wondering what to do, all of a sudden a lion appeared, fading in, like a shadow filling with life, and then it pounced on him! The lion rose on its hind legs and knocked him off balance. He dropped the gun and screamed as he was pushed up hard, with a great thud, against the door, the windows rattling from the force, then to the floor, the lion on top of him! He screamed as I never heard a person, a man scream before, begging for me to "get it off, get it off!" I stood, plastered to the wall, flabbergasted. Then Chuck and Lynn emerged from the bedroom, running at full speed from around the corner, Chuck with a gun in his hand, alarmed, into the living room. They stopped dead in their tracks a few feet away, seeing the lion pinning Jimmy to the floor! The lion then turned and looked at Chuck, the gun dangling at his side, and then it slowly faded and disappeared Jimmy continued to scream hysterically on the floor saying it was crushing him! Then Chuck, gathering his wits, finally moved forward after the animal disappeared. He picked his friend up off the floor, pulling him away from the spot he was attacked, and had Lynn cull me into the kitchen. Nothing was said, except a few expletives, but Chuck and Lynn protected me from Jimmy throughout the night and made sure I had safe passage home in the morning.

As of this writing, I am now 43 years old; I have not seen the lion, physically since that incident. I know he is still there, in moments I can feel its presence, and also feel a mate flanking my other side. Medicine men (Shaman) see it immediately in their spiritual sight. I am confident the lion will always be there when I need him, protecting me if ever threatened.

Chapter Four

Squirrel Thoughts

Growing up, seeing ghosts and visions and other strange phenomena was something I thought everybody was aware of and experienced, until I became an adolescent. It was normal for me to be able to watch an animal, squirrels being a particular favorite, and "throw" my mind into their body: I'd become a squirrel running along the trees, feeling what it was like to be a furry critter, somehow "attaching" my consciousness alongside and jointly experiencing its world. The first time I recall being able to do this was around eight years old. My family was living on Chamberlain Avenue, still in Little Ferry, NJ in a yellow cape-cod style house. I believe I was in detention in my bedroom. Staring out of my bedroom window through the pink lace curtains Mom had made, I watched a squirrel scurry up a tree and then sit a few yards away, eating a nut, seemingly having a good time. I really wanted to be in its place, and allowed my consciousness to rise up from me as I lay relaxing near the window. I could feel myself, a part of myself, floating across my backyard, seeing Andrew, our boarder, in the shed; one couldn't see the shed from my room, as it face out from the house into the yard.

There was a feeling, a sensation of electricity, which came from the attraction pulling me over to the squirrel. I hovered; I guess you can say, nearby, getting closer and closer. The closer I got, the more I could sense the squirrel's life force, the rapid beating of its heart and the quickness of its breathing. As I got closer to its furry little body, I sensed it was a male. It even had little squirrel thoughts that somehow became translated into a language I could understand. It seemed like a cheerful little fellar, and then I found myself attached inside it, like a magnet sticks to metal... I could hear and feel its thoughts and intentions, and feel the wind brushing our fur, and understand an 'other' dimension of communication, spoken through its tail, mostly. Apparently, the twitches of the tail were also a language; most other critters familiar with squirrels understood. Cool! I went for a wonderful, wild ride along the tree branches and leaves, sticking to whatever its paws landed on, like a cat. I don't know how long we were together, but the little fellar seemed to know I was there and didn't mind. I was invited to come around anytime.

I discovered growing up psychic that when I wanted to learn to run fast, I sought out a deer, and allowed that special attracting force to draw me into its being, and feel how its body moved; which muscles to engage for endurance, how to breathe, etc. It worked out well! I was the fastest runners in my township, I had to be, being chased half the time but thugs and snots with nothing better to do than pick on the town weirdo.

Chapter Five

Shape shifting, Astral projection and Dreaming

There appears to be delicate nuances between a shape shifting experience and astral projection. The similarities are that one releases consciousness from the physical body. Please, bear with me as I explain. It's interesting, the sensations of being attached, to another being fully cognizant of myself, without a physical form, and then submerged into sentience as I settled within my target; emotions were also there, as I experienced what it is to be a squirrel or bird or deer, and each animals' specific awareness of its' surroundings. I understand now that this ability is called, "shape shifting".

Reorienting with my physical body is almost instantaneous, unlike the projection of my consciousness or perhaps spirit, where an intense directing of intention and focus is required. I needed to allow/surrender to that magnetic, electric attraction pulling and drawing me to the target, when projecting myself into an animal. By contrast, slipping back into my body required no effort. I believe on some occasions the occurrence of shape shifting was an aspect of astral projection. That is the ability to separate your consciousness from your body. The process is subtle in many ways: I would completely relax my body as though I was going to sleep, allowing my mind to drift and float right to the brink of being totally focused inward, like beginning to enter into a dream state. Right before that point of becoming immersed into a dream, I would become awake, but my body would be deeply relaxed, to the point I almost didn't feel it. I would then try to wiggle inside, feeling my foot rise without moving it, or look to the left or right without moving my head. Then, a moment would come when I could roll over onto my side without moving a muscle, and slide out and stand beside my body. I found it a good idea to simply glance back at my still body. Sometimes something occurred where I was pulled or snapped back instantly inside my body; I would feel a sensation of weight, and couldn't slip back out. There is some sort of attachment, perhaps the 'silver cord' one hears about? People from all walks of life and throughout recorded history report that, when they find their consciousness separated from the physical body, whether in dream or projection, a silver cord is attached to both bodies; the essence and physical expression. I wasn't aware of the concept at the time; I only knew my experiences.

There is a different dynamic in shape shifting, which is the ability to turn yourself into another form, such as an animal, and astral projection which is somewhat like tagging along for the ride, being a passenger along another being, at least as far as I know.

To slip out of my body is an ability I have always known. As an infant, I can recall the sensation of my entire body relaxing, and from that point I would roll out of my body, following the line of my crib mattress, easily passing through the wooden bars to the floor and pop back up and walk/float around the house. I would check on my family as they slept, or performed whatever activities they happened to be up to. In the kitchen area there was a portal, and just on the other side of it I would meet up with a guide or guardian angel and we would move from beyond the house to an 'otherwhere' as I still call it, and have adventures. We traveled to many different places, about which I was curious, places I perhaps spotted during the day. At times, I would visit with people I knew there, but would instantly forget as soon as I passed back through the portal, back to my room and still body. The memories are vivid yet veiled, as best as I can describe it, like attempting to recover images from a dream in its entirety.

I found out there were a lot of things other people couldn't do, that were natural to me. I enjoyed this multifaceted plane. In my dreams, I learned to run, take a big jump, and leap over a gated fence, becoming airborne and able to control my flight. I could also ride my bike, peddling very, very fast, again toward some sort of necessary jump, and lift off. I had to be precise in my intentions; otherwise I couldn't get off the ground. It is like I have to trust, once I reached a certain point that I will lift off the ground and soar. This type of dream was different from the others. There are layers somehow, or perhaps levels more apropos, on the other side of waking consciousness, and this kind of dream, I was awake but dreaming. The world can be a lot more interesting without the laws of physics or gravity!

I'd explore places in dreams, through astral travel, around my home town and surrounding areas that I would later visit when awake. This not only validated my experiences, but also helped me discover places I never knew existed beyond my small range as a kid. I now understand this to be called lucid dreaming...it's the greatest place in the world!
I also wonder if it is also an aspect of 'remote viewing'?

Chapter Six

Hard Lessons

I explored and discovered different levels of reality freely until the age of eleven-ish. It was then that it was strongly stated to me that all this "stuff" didn't exist. It wasn't right, period. There weren't any ghosts or anything beyond the visible world! Dreams were just that, dreams, and anything else a coincidence!

That bit of information came from a grade school teacher, one that I respected and loved dearly. She became scared after I warned her one day to be careful around her car. She asked what I meant, by around her car? I told her she was going to have a bad accident around her car. She cajoled me and said that what I was saying was non-sense!

A few days later, it happened. She was walking to her car in a parking lot. A large truck had parked next to her and as she went to open the drivers' side door of her VW bug, the truck driver, unable to see her, smacked her hard across the head with the bottom of his door. The impact caused a serious gash and instantly knocked her unconscious. She remained hospitalized for quite a while.

She fully recovered from the concussion and stitches, but our relationship was never the same. She became frightened of me! Her attitude was very difficult to deal with. She chose to ignore and avoid me. Eventually she transferred to another school, though; I don't believe it was because of our relationship.

My teacher's words impressed me deeply. One cannot deny experience, though.

I truly respected my teacher, who had helped me so much. Her assertions though, confused me. I knew through personal experience one did have thoughts inside them I could see as pictures, sometimes as beams of light strands radiating from their body, and describe in detail those thoughts, dwelling within their minds, ruminated upon, and things never spoken aloud. There are ghosts and spirits hanging around people, whom I thought were ignored! My experiences were in direct opposition to what many around me considered possible. Reality was pretty narrow to those around me. Even if the information I related was accurate, it seemed easier for people to dismiss rather than embrace. An enigmatic conflict grew in my mind slowly.

A transforming idea was expressed by one of the spirits I would chat with to whom I had posed serious questions about how it is that, people were willing to discount or completely dismiss what is not understood, even in the face of reality?
The reply I received was that people actually had a choice to accept or deny certain aspects of reality, even their own experiences!

This began a journey into the curiosities' of the nature of Mind, and the study of all the dynamics of the Nature of realities. Science is the study of that which can be observed, described, and be replicated, true?

As far as I understand it, truth must be demonstrated. I became a student and lay scientist that day. I was personally skeptical anyway, until the information I received or experiences I had were validated. Now, I sought other people's experience. I knew I wasn't alone; I had books of ghost stories... The library was an excellent place to explore. One could go into a section of interest and find many publications or areas never before known. I learned the word, 'paranormal' and about ESP (extrasensory perception).

The school I had attended, with the teacher who impressed me so profoundly, taught me how to stand on my own two feet. If you want something, you must make a solid decision, and then accomplish your desire. I learned how to research and cross reference. The library on Liberty Street for a time throughout my youth became not unlike a friendship. I even thought at one point of becoming a librarian, so I would always have the latest information. Hours passed by in the blink of an eye as I found out about people with similar experiences. I learned of other talents like psychokinesis; moving objects with thoughts, and commenced to practice here and there. Slowly, I was also learning how to control my abilities.

My teacher taught me an important lesson; Keep your mouth shut! Her reaction and withdrawal of affections hurt. I was somewhat used to being shunned by other kids, but not by a loved one. We were close, and people even thought we looked like mother and daughter! I discovered I needed to be very careful with whom I shared psychic information with, and the art of discernment, or the recognition between what others actually verbalized, and internal thoughts kept to themselves. Also, "preterknowledge"; Knowledge of what is to enact.

Growing up psychic doesn't mean I was always "on". There were many times I "shined" brightly, in a manner Stephen King describes in his novel, "The Shinning". I like the description in that there are moments I am cognizant of an intense energetic field chock full of information, and other times I am "dull" to it. Sometimes I shielded myself from it, the energy, so to speak, as if I were turning down the volume on a radio or simply switching off or shutting down. I noticed it was difficult, and still is, to turn down the volume when I am sick, especially during a fever. Being ill presents an annoying ability to hear energy, electricity and airwaves/radio frequencies and color television sets. It was only useful when I desired to freak someone out or play with their heads and tell them to turn to this station, my favorite song such n such is playing...Over and over. I could be mischievous at times! As an adult, I came across an article in a periodical that described this, calling it, "ultrasonic hearing" and claimed that Barbara Streisand has it. Finally, I found a reference. I have never spoken to Ms. Streisand about it, though.

Chapter Seven

The Witch

Living in the small town of Little Ferry, New Jersey in the 1960's, and growing up the town weirdo or witch was not easy. I became one of the fastest runners in Bergen County! There were many occasions kids would seemingly befriend me, just to ridicule and make fun of me in front of their friends. I would get hit or punched, rocks thrown at me from kids taunting me from atop their bicycles.

As many gifts within myself I explored, there was one very vital talent absent, knowing if a person was lying to me or being sincere. (Being human, I have been taught to ignore instincts)

One day, a boy about nine years old, blond and slightly stocky approached me, risking losing all his peers if seen in public with me. I was crossing an empty parking lot, and he ran up to me and asked, "Where is my lost puppy?" I said, "I don't have your puppy." He said, "But you know where it is!" "No", I protested, confused, "I've never even met you!" He insisted that I knew and, on the verge of tears asked me to please tell him where the puppy was? "Here", he said, then thrust out his hand that held a quarter up in the air. He said, "If you tell me where my puppy is, I will give you this money," placing it in my hand. I was reluctant, but empathetic.

The posing of a question automatically 'switched on' the Knowing ability... I said, "I see a picture in my mind that you were in a swamp area last, with the puppy. Your Mom told you not to play there because of the snakes, quite a way from your home." This freaked him out as he nodded his head "yes..." I said, "The puppy will be found a half block from your house at 3pm."

His eyes flew open wide, and then he yelled, "That's not true, he's lost in the swamp!" The boy then punched me in the chest, and took his quarter back. He hit me hard, and I began to cry. I already had plans on getting two chocolate bars with the fortune of money.

The boy ran off, and I went about my business, tears drying on my cheeks. The next day he actually came to my house, knocked on the front door, again a bold move, and gave me the quarter back! I asked him what it was for, waiting to be hit again. He said, "A neighbor had found the puppy wandering in the street, half a block from his house, and returned it at 3pm." Then he quickly turned around and ran away. I never saw the boy again and now, I was called, "WITCH!" everywhere I went. So, needless to say, I didn't have many friends.

I feel greatly fortunate to have grown up in a time when kids were expected to attend school, check in with a parent, change into play clothes, and get home by suppertime. It left many hours to wander and discover. Northern New Jersey in the 1960's had dense clusters of people and homes, yet still had wilds of forests, and swamps, and marshes, and neighbors who watched out for one another.

Now, I didn't necessarily care for the neighbors' watchfulness; if I was spotted where I wasn't supposed to be, invariably a "neighbor" would call my Mother and rat me out! Mom would remind me not to wander too far away from home or go near the swamps and marshes, there were snakes, including poisonous copperheads, muskrats, and other critters that were dangerous. As she related the dangers to me, I could feel it; visceral electricity would travel through my body, as though there were a dual layer of understanding from what she said, thought, and to that which she had an emotional reaction. My Father, on the other hand, felt corporal discipline was the way to deal with any consideration of a challenge, of disobedience or to question his authority! We become the parents who raised us, and Father was raised in such a way.

One day I begged to go outside to play at a local park a block or so from the house, as Mom prepared dinner. Mom relented (being under foot) but told me not to go beyond the park, and to come back at dusk, or when I see Dad's car go by on his way home from work. Cheerfully, I shot out the door and headed for the swings. I had the park all to myself, which was a treat, and enjoyed pumping high into the air on the swings, becoming weightless for a mili-second. On one of the passes, I spied something shiny on the ground. I leaped off the swing from the highest point I could, and plopped down in the dirt, keeping my feet. I located the spot I had seen glistening, and found a quarter! A great fortune, being a kid! A quarter bought at least two chocolate bars or a hand-full of penny candies!

I was so hungry, it being close to dinner time, so I decided to go to the candy store on the corner a couple of blocks away. When I made this decision, I felt a weight upon my gut, accompanied by a very strong feeling inside that I am doing something wrong. That was, and still is a special sensation. Anytime I made a seriously wrong decision, this intense sense/sensation and feeling deep in my stomach would shadow over me. An indescribable pressure physically, warned me of impending doom. The feeling was a combination of an instinct we all have, along with a psychic sense of foreboding. Learning to discern the difference between instinct, intuition, and a layering of both would take a great many years!

With each step, I remembered what Mom said, to not go beyond the park, but she wasn't near, she would never know I disobeyed her. Being very hungry and enticed by the temptation of something sweet, I took my chances and quickened my steps. I went to Sam's Spot, the candy store on the corner, spent my found money, and then quickly headed back to the park. As the sun set, I ran back home for dinner. When I entered the house, my Dad confronted me and asked where I had been. Feeling very threatened, I said, "I've been at the park." He said, "oh yeah, then why did a neighbor call and say she saw you leave the park and went to the store?" and I began to tell him what happened. Before all the words left my lips, I was whisked up under his arm and brought to the bathroom. He told me to pull my pants down and wait for him as he angrily left the bathroom, closing the door behind him. I knew what that meant. A beating! I panicked. Scared out of my mind I ran around the tiny room as I heard him getting the leather belt. I had to pee, but just before I could relieve myself, he came back into the room. He grabbed me and threw me over his knee, holding me down draped across his legs. I don't recall how many lashes I received as I was screamed at; I only know it was long and brutal enough that I couldn't hold my bladder, and peed all over him! That, of course, did not make the situation any better, and got a few more sturdy lashes with that very stiff and sturdy dark leather belt. I was so sore; I was unable to sit for dinner. Eventually I was sent to my room and I sobbed myself to sleep.

Dad had a heavy hand, or rather, leather belt! There was a reason for the action, a lesson taught by being beaten, as it were.

I was loved by my Father, he taught me how to ride a bike, he cherished me, and on occasion he given me a treasure of wisdom: "Measure twice, cut once." I have found this can be applied to nearly every situation one may encounter in the world.

I became very aware of my environment from that day forward. I chose places to hang out where I could not be seen. Obscure areas discovered through my astral travels, away from tattletale telling eyes!

Through the need to hide, I became more energetically aware of my surroundings, environment, and developed the sensing of people witnessing me, being aware of my presence, like, knowing I came on a persons' radar. I worked on the abilities of invisibility. I do not mean literally invisible, but energetically. One can learn to sort of "cloak" their presence. The trick is to have no emotion. Fear and attachment is the biggest difficulty to conquer! As long as you do not fear, or have a great deal of excitement, you can move through life un-noticed. This ability as well needed to be honed. Life, I have found, requires a balance, which is not static. A strength can become a liability, if one is not flexible. A weakness can create an opening within perception, or a (ideological) position in need of a specific acuity, in mind, and sometimes acquiescence. The discovery of energies that intersect the physical world and soul, intertwined, are a constant: If you grow up psychic. *See Appendix B

Eight

A discovery and a Deed

As I learned to travel through backyards and around the edges of forested areas, I discovered intriguing places. On one such foray, not too far from a local fishing pond call Indian Lake, I aimlessly wandered through a neighborhood I had never been in before. I noticed that as I went further up the street, the road appeared to end. Being curious, I followed the road as it inclined in a soft grade, until it ended, well, sort of. The street then curved, allowing vehicles to veer to the left, or right. In front of me was what looked like an island of overgrown bushes, and lots of trees; it was a hill, rising above street level, with lots of birdsong. As I walked along the perimeter of a seemingly impenetrable thicket, I thought I heard voices. I listened closer, and definitely heard people speaking. Then a voice, sounding like a young boy said, "come on over!" with an accent, possibly southern? I wasn't sure what to make of the request, being used to being told to go away! But the voice, sounding like another kid, seemed pleasant enough. At first, I couldn't find a way through the thick tangled growth of vegetation; then I got on my hands and knees and found a way under the bushes. Cool!

I went in a few feet until I could stand. I found a wonderful oasis! I walked a bit up a hill, though I couldn't see the people talking. I could still hear soft voices around me. I yelled out asking, "Where are you?" and received a response, "over here!" I moved in the direction from which the voice came, but still couldn't see anyone. This created an intrigue, a curiosity within me. As I explored further, I noticed long, white, rounded stones on the ground. I thought it was perhaps a dumping ground. As I moved towards the echoes, I noticed more white stones, some sticking out of the ground, others erect. Then, examining them closer, I could make out faint writing barely indented on them; they were grave markers! Way Cool!

As I checked out these strange headstones, observed that these were very, very old:
Cora, 1879-1894
Nora Reed, died July 29, 1902 aged 17 years
Cornelia J. Smith, died Aug 15, 1866 aged 1 yr 11 mo 6 ds
Wow, a baby! This somehow brought me to my senses. I no longer heard the soft voices, and, funny, the birds were silent. Actually, there was no noise! I was a little spooked, and suddenly aware that the sun was getting low, and that it was cold. I called out one more time to the voice that had asked me to 'come on over', but there was no response. I decided to leave, as it was becoming cooler and cooler. I made my way back near the spot where I had entered and, on my hands and knees, crawled back out. As I stood up, I noticed how warm it was. Strange, I thought. Also, the sounds of traffic were now prevalent. I walked around the edge of

this tree island and discovered a busy thoroughfare, full of late afternoon traffic on the other side. Funny how, inside the island it had been totally silent! I decided to go back early the next day, to explore more.
I did return, day after day, exploring the cemetery. I enjoyed this place, recognizing that once I entered the grounds, all sounds disappeared. There was no litter, not even a soda can!

Okay, we are speaking of the early 1970's. The world was a dirty, filthy place. Cars did not have emission standards, and people thought the earth was their garbage can. They began to teach in school: "Give A Hoot, Don't Pollute!" just around this time. Anybody remember the oil embargo? There were long lines of automobiles, waiting for hours to fuel up. The numbers at the end of the license plate determined if a vehicle could fill the tank with gasoline. (To deal with the hours, sometimes days' of long lines at the gas station, the state decided to implement an "odd/even days", which meant; if your license plate ended in an odd or even number, you could buy gas, which I believe correlated to the day of the week, if there was any gas left by the time you got to the pump!) Environmentalism was in its infancy. I couldn't walk along the shores of the Hudson River without masses of debris floating by, piled on the banks, unknown gray-white frothy foaming stuff that may have been a new life form emerging from the scum, like something out of the "Creature Feature" television show that aired horror movies. It was a serious mess!
The graveyard though, seemed completely untouched

by pollution. Every time I entered the graveyard, I called out to see if the stranger was there that day. Then, one day I received a response! The same, "over here" beckon came back, but I could never find him! Finally one day I called out and he called back and said, "Over here!" I said, "I'm over here, come on over!" and he did! Slowly, timidly, a boy made his way over to me. He was dressed in odd clothing, and I asked where did he get them from? He said, "My maw made them for me," and seemed very proud. We talked for a while, and I realized he was a spirit! He said his name was Billy. He was so engaging that I really didn't notice he was not 'real'. I was so excited to have someone interested in chatting and hanging out with me. From that day forward, we agreed to meet when I visited the 'island'. We enjoyed a friendship over the next couple of months. One day, Billy asked, "Why are you different?" I asked, "What do you mean? He said, "When I touched you, I am full of buzzing," he couldn't describe it. It slipped out of my mouth and I said, "it could be because you are dead, Billy." "Dead?" he asked. He whipped around and said, "What!?" I repeated myself saying, "You are a ghost Billy." He thought I was joking! I said, "No," and then I asked him to walk with me to a gravestone. He followed me apprehensively, and I paused in front of a grave stone that had names on both sides of the marker. I asked, "isn't your real name 'Willet'?" He said, "Yes, but nobody calls me that, it's Billy." Then I asked, "Are the names on the headstone your family?" He said, "I can't read," so, I read the names aloud"

"Henry White died May 23, 1911." He said, "I don't

know that name." Then I read the backside of the stone; "George, Leah Anne, Amos, Clarence, Willet." He said, "Those are my brothers and sister!" I asked, "What happened? Why are you all dead?"
He stood there for a long time. It began to get colder and colder. He had a lot of trouble remembering. I asked, "Who was your favorite family?" Immediately he said, "My brother George, he is my best friend, and taught me how to shoe a horse!" I asked, "Where is your brother now?" Then he paused. It became very light, like a thousand suns beamed down on us and he turned towards me and said, "thank you, thank you, I can see my brother, that's my brother!" and disappeared!

The light went away, and it was cool again. Inside, I knew I just lost a friend, my only friend. I went home and just went to bed. I didn't even have supper, instead pretending to be asleep when called to the table. I knew he (went) gone away, but I still called whenever I returned to the cemetery. Billy and I had both spoken of the echoing, soft voices; he heard them, too, but never could find the source.

One day as I made my way to my private place, the abandoned cemetery, I met a reporter along Indian Lake. We struck up a conversation. I told him I had to leave before it got too late. He asked, "Where are you going?" I said, "The old cemetery up the street." He said, "There isn't one up the street, but a few blocks over, you know, where the road curves to the right." I said, "There is," and began to describe it, revealing my secret place. He was intrigued and asked, "May I go with you?" I said, "Sure, if you don't give away my secret." He agreed and I brought him to my refuge from the world. As he looked around, he was amazed. This was a discovery! He began to snap pictures as I showed him the dates and half buried weather-worn headstones. It wasn't too long after that that an article appeared in the local paper about a forgotten burial ground on Moonachie road. I no longer had a private sanctuary; I had been betrayed! I lost my place of solace as activity now surrounded the graveyard re-discovery.

As I researched this memory for verifiable facts, I became aware through contacting the local newspapers, primarily The Record, that many generations had "discovered" the forgotten graveyard. My Father also mentioned his generation used to gather up there as teenagers. They would party and drink. As the years passed he said, "It became a cess-pool, littered with bottles, and tires and old shopping carts." Odd, I thought. Whenever I visited, it was littered with tall prairie grasses, wildflowers and grave markers in various states of wear.

There is an on-going dispute as to who actually owns this very valuable piece of land. The 'island', is an acre separating a thoroughfare, Route 46 veering to the left, and quiet streets of suburbia, stretching off to the right.

Little RED house on Maiden Lane

Swamp

Bergen County — It I

[G]raves Unkept [I]n Little Ferry

By LINDA HOLMES

LITTLE FERRY — An old [ce]metery next to the Route 46-[Li]berty Street intersection is [no]w a burial ground for junk.

Established in 1860 as a [ce]metery for blacks, many of [th]e ancient gravestones are [no]w hidden in some spots by [fi]ve-foot weeds. Other stones [a]re so weathered that names [a]re no longer distinguishable.

"Most slave and freedmen's [g]rave[s] were marked only with [a] chunk of sandstone or other [co]mmon rock, perhaps with [it]s corners squared off," said [Jo]seph Zodl, member of the [B]ergen County Historical So[ci]ety. Several of these sites [h]ave now disintegrated into [th]e natural terrain.

But today it is also hard to [fi]nd the stones of granite and [po]lished marble. Beer cans, [a]n old stove, part of a car, [tr]ee limbs, and other rubbish [hi]de the graves.

About eight months ago, the [B]ergen County Historical So[ci]ety decided not to restore [th]e cemetery, said Zodl. They [w]ere more interested in other [co]unty sites.

Borough Clerk John Bacik [sa]id a youth group had offered [to] clean up the cemetery last year, but now he can't find the group.

"I'd like to clean it up, but help is hard to find," said Bacik.

At one time Mayor Malcolm W. Hill had hoped the borough could obtain the property, but no direct survivor of the original land trustees were found.

Several suggestions have been made for future use of the land, which range from declaring it an historical s[ite] to using it as the westbou[nd] lane of the state highway i[nto] Liberty Street.

The site was My Favor[ite] Eyesore for two Record rea[d]ers.

Staff Photo by Richard Zimmerman

LOST CEMETERY — A headstone in a burial ground is almost obscured by foliage.

Old Cemetery Eyed For Use As Road

MAY 19 1965

Acre Could Solve Traffic Problem, But Borough Can't Find Owner

Little Ferry — A cemetery for Negroes that was created [i]n the days when Hackensack was known as New Barbadoes [i]s being eyed by the Borough Council for municipal use.

Residents of the Borough have [b]een aware for years that the [1]-acre plot on the northeast [c]orner of Liberty Street and [R]oute 46 is unoccupied, run-[d]own, and apparently unowned.

The Council has received sev[e]ral requests from residents [th]at the owners of the property [b]e required to spruce up the [p]remises. A title search by Bor[o]ugh Attorney Robert S. Krause [w]as unfruitful, Krause said last [n]ight.

He reported that the prem[is]es were sold Nov. 17, 1860 by [Jo]hn B. Marshall and his wife, [M]ary Ann, of Lodi to John J. [D]emarest, G. Myers Anderson, [an]d Simeon Zabriskie, leading [ci]tizens of New Barbadoes, who [cr]eated a trust to establish a [c]emetery for the Negroes of [th]e Village of Hackensack.

Krause said the property [w]ould belong to the heirs of the [la]st survivor of the original [tr]ustees, whose identity is un[k]nown because of inadequate [r]ecords before 1900.

The attorney said the munic[ipality] could acquire the land by condemnation, providing the bodies now in the cemetery were removed and buried elsewhere.

The property is still privately owned at present, so the Borough cannot expend public funds to clean up or maintain the 1-acre plot, Krause said.

Mayor Fred A. Heinige said he thought the Boy Scouts could undertake the cleanup project as a community service.

Councilman Jerry Vozeh said he would like to see the land acquired by the State and used for a traffic bypass to ease congestion at the intersection of Liberty Street and Route 46.

Vozeh said that the plot is located ideally to provide a special channel from the slow westbound lane of the State highway into Liberty Street. Thus, drivers desiring to make either a left or right turn from the westbound lane would do so from the slow lane. This would remove a major traffic block and safety hazard, Vozeh said.

Chapter Nine

Seeing Thoughts

My cousin Robin and her family, minus Uncle Tracey, moved into Little Ferry from the Southern shore of New Jersey when we were about ten years old. I was delighted, and we each had an instant friend! We had always liked each other, and were only six months apart in age. One summer afternoon I was leaving her house on my way home. Carefully descending the twenty-five or so steep wooden steps that led away from her second floor apartment, I noticed a young woman walking on the opposite side of the street; approaching from down the block in the direction I was headed. She must have been all of 19 -20 years old, blond, cute, wearing the hippy fashion of the day; her hair long and loose with a few thin braids around her faced. She wore a light, colorful peasant-type shirt and hip-hugger bell-bottom jeans. As sometimes occurred, I spontaneously 'picked up' on her thoughts. Sometimes, I would see an internal movie within my mind. Or, a bunch of still-like photos in an order that my logic could not wrap around; yet that told a story. Sometimes, I saw projected energy from a person's head, and entire body. They looked like illuminated 'strings', or beams of light streaming from, but somehow though, and looping around, yet moving outward from people. Each 'string' had a multi-layered thought, with many, many nuances. Sometimes, I just 'knew' information, what I have come to term; "Pure knowing." This I didn't perfect until much later on in my twenties.

Slowly, step by step, as I moved further down the narrow stairs to the sidewalk, I stumbled across a thought, as her brain rattled on, I just couldn't understand. My mind and brain puzzled and puzzled, probing deeper into her thoughts, trying to find the answer. She was thinking, "after I get the laundry, fix dinner, I'm gonna jump into my boyfriends pants." I thought, "Why would she want to do that?" She had great bell-bottoms on. Besides, getting a visual of her boyfriend from her mind, he was much larger than she, and they wouldn't fit! Deeper and deeper, I scanned her. As I reached the bottom step, I found it, the information. Oh boy did I find it! I didn't know anything about that stuff! I was somewhat horrified and embarrassed. I realized that this was very personal information! In that moment I decided my teacher may have been right, this isn't right.

But, I took it differently than intended perhaps. To this day I am reluctant to scan someone without their consent. Embarrassments mainly taught me this lesson, a few times over, as described below:

Around ten or eleven years old I was browsing in a store. There were a bunch of people shopping and going through the aisles. A young boy had passed by me, and instantly, I knew absolutely, that he intended to steal something. This, "knowing" was so strong, like a pungent odor, it distracted me from the item I was looking at. "A radio" entered my mind. I looked up and over to the brown haired, brown eyed boy. I also became aware, on an energetic level that, the boy was being watched, by the store clerk. I rushed up to him and said quietly, "they're watching you, don't take that transistor radio, you'll get caught." The boys' eyes flew open, wide, staring straight into mine and said, "How do you know that?" I said, "Be careful." We both understood each other, in that seemingly suspended moment.

He freaked, and ran like a bolt of lightning towards the door. As he stepped outside, two men grabbed him and demanded he give back the stolen items. They spun him around, and in a flash, the men then proceeded to search through his pockets, in front of the shoppers in the store. They didn't find anything. The men seemed perplexed, sure he had taken something. The kid took a quick look back at me, still frightened. But, I could sense relief spilling from behind his brown eyes, and then went on his way.

It was a lonely way to grow up, being different. It wasn't just the 'witchy' part, being considered a weirdo. But also, in my hometown school, kids still remembered me, from years ago. From kindergarten through third grade I had what I thought was a good friend, Peter. When I began attending middle school back in my home town after a few years of being bused out to another district, he pointed me out to his friends, reminding them of how I used to be. I was just becoming a regular kid in their eyes, not openly shunned. I was naturally shy, and it only intensified not being accepted, yet again.

But, I had trees, and forests and creeks, pronounced, 'cricks'. I loved to fish at Indian Lake, a pond really, situated at the edge of a park I couldn't go too. Someone was always willing to chase me away or harass me in some way. I was not invited to play 'reindeer games'. The pond had a history of swallowing human life and carriages. Allegedly, early in the town's beginnings a carriage, with a man and a woman were driven into the pond to their deaths. The horses drawing the carriage were spooked, bolting right to the pond's edge of earth meeting water, and sunk beneath the waters, before anyone could reach the couple inside. The driver went down with the ship, as it were, entangled by the reins. Or the truck; making a delivery, the driver hit the corner too fast and landed at the water's edge, the quicksand in minutes sucking the entire truck and trailer down, the driver barely escaping. Urban legend said: "Once past between 1-5ft marks is where the quicksand started."

The entire area of New Jersey was known for these quicksand traps... if you didn't know where they were, there may be peril. This is my understanding as a kid, and kept me on my toes, as I explored the natural marshes. I loved cattails, and towering reeds, things

growing above me.
Indian Lake was also legendary for its snapping turtles. Some idiot, "a few years back" as the story goes, released three baby snapping turtles into the pond, transplanted from nearby marshes. They grew and snipped the arms off of unsuspecting kids pausing along its shores! I was never certain if it was a local legend to keep kids from wading or swimming in the treacherous pond or, if it truly happened, I kept my eyes open though!

I fished as often as possible, particularly after school, for sunfish and trout during the week, having most of the place to myself. Other kids had the fortune of engaging in a group activity, such as baseball or just hanging out with friends. My friends were trees and fishing.

When I wasn't able to fish, I spent time trying 'on' different animals, and also discovered that *anything* virtually, could be 'tried on'. To experience, what I can only describe loosely as, what I'll call 'sensations', as I experimented with shape shifting, or projecting my consciousness into a tree, and join with it's being. The sensation of feeling the temperate breeze, blowing through leaves: Richly aware, of each individual leaf. I experienced each leaf-self swaying and twirling, also simultaneously aware of a sense of expansion, yielding to natures; forces. For some extraordinary moments, I became, or merged energetically, with the trees' trunk and boughs balancing: our/my roots, penetrating deep into the ground, holding fast. The travels through different layers of earth and sands and rocks spreading off through surrounding areas, the coolness of underground waters, yet, it wasn't the sensation or feeling of cold, it is like there is a texture to temperature. There was such an intimate and rich connection, and, awareness of, of everything around me at several levels of frequency. Merging with this tree, there was even a sort of communication with other creatures and trees. Amazing!

I had an experience many years later with a tree in Oak lawn, Il outside of Chicago. I am walking with my friend Tony near dusk in Wolff Wildlife Refuge. We were deep in conversation when I paused for a moment, leaning my left hand upon a tree, resting. The tree then communicated a story of its life and also of its future life, when it would become charcoal for a human campfire, when humans would be few and far between! It was like, a magnetic connection, my consciousness, my mind being drawn into, into a memory not my own. I knew the sentience of being a tree, though from many years ago. It was like I was pulled in, and then, popped back out with a literal experience of jumping in and out of something; of time, it was reminiscent of an energetic portal, an experience! I turned to Tony, completely surprised, and shared what had just happened... He seen the peace and shock on my face, and knew something happened! Tony and I had many psychic and energetic adventures together. Our relationship will be explored and explained in subsequent chapters of volume 2.

I also had the experience of being a blade of grass, with a bug walking along my form. Absolutely a kinesthetic, sensorial experience! My favorite thing to do was to lie deep in the prairie grasses and wildflowers that grew 4-5ft tall, being able to hide from life for a while, watch clouds and then project myself way up high, and see them from the inside. It was my first ride on an airplane that reminded and validated my knowledge of what a cloud looks like from the inside or above. The billowing towers of vapor rose high into space. There were colors rippling throughout them that were so soft and transient, melding and merging seamlessly. Sometimes I witnessed jets of lightning shooting upward towards space in variants of colors. They blinked and splashed over the tops of clouds without sound, only electricity. Way cool! It wasn't until the 1990's that these energy bursts were accepted by mainstream science. Watching the Discovery Channel one day, I found out that pilots would report seeing them, but had no proof of what they had witnessed. I think a satellite finally captured images, which were categorized as "jets" and "spurts."

If I was bored in school, I would fix my focus on the teacher. Then I worked on being able to see around the space I occupied, without moving my head. Once this was achieved, I then slipped out of my body and played in the field outside the classroom or I would go home and hang out. I wasn't always easy to punish, either. If I was sent to my room for misbehaving, I would lie on my bed, slip out of my body and sit on the stairs, and watch television anyway! I'll never forget

watching Tom Jones. He was a singer and entertainer who had a weekly show. He performed, “What’s new pussycat” one particular evening, when I was being punished, I watched in awe as he sweated profusely as he sang and pranced throughout the number. I remembered being disgusted by the sweat that spewed from him, dissolving in front of the cameras, as underwear was tossed on stage, yuck!
I should have stayed in my room that night. No offense Tom.

My abilities were not under my complete control. I was learning along the way and through the years through trial and error. I had to learn how things worked, ‘at will’, which for some talents were easy, like slipping out of my body, and difficult for others, like accessing information I wanted. It was as if the information or knowledge was cropped and shown only fragments. An incomplete picture can be quite confusing in many ways, perhaps more so when one doesn’t know what the image is, but a feeling accompanies each intuition, creating layers one is not able to comprehend at certain ages. The mind can only wrap itself around so much.

Being somewhat sad, lonely, and angry adjusted or narrowed the field, the type of information I would pick up, let’s say, ethereally. I knew when plane crashes would occur, when people died, and things of that nature. I didn’t know in my youth that, one’s attitude and emotional outlook directly correlated to the type of ‘vision’ or information one could access. It actually compounded my problems!

I knew and felt the distress of others empathically and psychically, especially if I was close emotionally. It was like I had my own emotions to deal with, as well as those of others going through challenges, fear and heartache. To have the knowledge/vision of a plane crashing and not able to do anything about it was frustrating to say the least. It took a long time to discover, how I felt about myself, and the information, information not knowledge, of the world in general. Conflict affected my psychic abilities.

The other inherent issue of growing up psychic is the disbursing of energy; that mimics an electric field. If I was upset or angry, light bulbs or stereo systems didn't last long; a lot of the time they would blow up! Most of the time a radio would work a few days later. At other times, smoke would come from the back and I knew it was fried! Throwing a light switch or touching a lamp would sometimes cause the bulb to "snap", the bulb would not explode, but would blink on and off, or become static-y, and then stop working. I didn't realize that I was throwing off emotional charges, psychic energy that caused these things to occur.

Imagine the effect of having a bad day; walk in my shoe's for just a moment: After everything has gone wrong all day, you return to the sanctity of your home, where flipping on the light switch causes the bulb to blow out so, now you have to tend to that; then the new bulb pops, giving up, you get something to drink, that spills, you trip up the stairs, and the ultimate finale; flushing the toilet and it floods.

I was a poltergeist!
(Physical law/universal law; 'like attracts like'. Perhaps each strength and weakness of all probabilities of potential was influenced energetically?)

Sometimes, a poltergeist is called an unruly spirit. Like most things in life, not all phenomena are 'fixed' in terms of explanation. It seems as though the world is made of black, and white, and shades of gray... much gray. Poltergeists come in several forms, as I understand the expressions, but primarily, they are of one of few sources; the first, is a troubled young person, an adolescent, who unknowingly throws off psychic charges of unprocessed, chaotic emotional energy, thus creating havoc, in the physical environment. Objects move of their own accord (psychokinesis) such as furniture sliding across the room, or things breaking. There is an actual physical phenomenon that family members and others can witness or even become a target. Along the lines of similar situations, environmental disturbances I suspect are very much related to the term coined 'poltergeist', such as rocks raining down on a particular house and other strange occurrences reported around the world.

Another form from which a poltergeist can present is as an angry 'spirit'. If perhaps someone enters into what is considered "their territory"; like, moving into a home of a former owner or spirit, one who had previously occupied the location, and continues to consider the home or area their property or private domain. The living persons are seen as intruders. Just like if some family barged into your home and took up residence, without an invitation or agreement, these earth-bound spirits will attempt through intimidation to rid their home or space of the intruders through acts that are called 'haunting'. The situation can become volatile and frightening for occupants of the home or area involved. Another expression of a poltergeist can emerge that is actually a troublesome entity, attracted to a household that wants to create disruption of the family to split them apart, thriving on negative energy. I use the term, "entity" because it is not as far as I am aware, the spirit of a passed-over human or animal, but another type of energy or force. These cases are rare.

Then there are other energies, those of an intense negative nature, very unpleasant, which are emotionally and physically ominous and threatening. I personally have found through experience and investigation that these negative energies emanate from living individual's confronting something. Within these individuals' psyches lies an unacknowledged, emotionally charged issue that is not contained within the confines of their mind, but energetically expressed. This is most often the case regarding poltergeist activity; however, there are no hard and fast rules.

Psychic occurrences can be very disquieting, and either provoke curiosity or fear in any particular individual. Imagine putting on a blindfold; the remaining four senses heighten to compensate for this major loss of information, sight. This may feel eerie or draw keen and acute attention. Flexibility of personality draws the line, and generally determines whether the experience itself will be positive or threatening.

Tony the Ghost on Chamberlain Avenue had a hand in teaching me lessons of personal control by his antics. Eventually, the experiences of living with Tony the Ghost, led me to discover and research my understanding of the nature of our shared realities, and motives.

Chapter Ten

Tony the Ghost

My parents divorced when I was around eight years old. We moved from the little red house on Maiden lane to a yellow Cape Cod style home a few miles away, on Chamberlain Avenue. Mom thought it was important that we have both parents, and chose to remain in the same town of Little Ferry, so we could visit our Dad. The new house had a full basement with an old fashioned furnace that had these large round ducts stretching out like an octopus' arms, wrapped in asbestos and metal straps. Quite a sight! It also had a secret hiding place, a cupboard under the basement stairs that a young child could fit into. Mom thought it was for storing quilts, sheets, and heavy winter blankets, but I knew better. My own personal fort!

The main floor had the traditional large kitchen, built -in sideboards with glass and wood door cabinets, painted white, with a breakfast nook, large enough to accommodate our six seat deep brown pine kitchen table which, marked by the passing years with scratches, carvings and the toll of 40 or so years of being handed down sits in my kitchen to this day.

An attached dining room with a swinging, solid maple door led around into the living room through a large opening 2/3rds the length of the wall. Beyond the living room was a sun room, with an open architectural arch at the front of the house, graciously dividing the two spaces. Large bay windows and tall spruce trees outside created a screened privacy, yet let in loads of light. Hardwood maple floor ran throughout the house, which I believed was built around the early 1900's. Steep carpeted stairs lead to the second floor, with a large rectangle opening in the interior wall halfway up the staircase that overlooked the living room. There were three bedrooms upstairs, with the smallest room that led to the full attic. I am sure the small room actually was a landing or vestibule, but the tiny space contained enough area for an intimate bedroom with two large windows. My Brother scored that room, which I envied. Mom, of course, had the master bedroom, which still had an old solid brass and spring bed frame, which had to have been a hundred years old by the time we moved in. It is still the most comfortable bed I ever had the pleasure to encounter. Mom's top mattress and a feather tic thick quilt, heaven! Each spring gave way to the contours of your body, engulfing and surrounding you like a cocoon. My sister and I drew the room adjacent to the one bathroom for the entire house, and closest to the stairs at the top of the landing. Our room, like all the others, had huge windows from which we could see the ancient oak trees in the backyard, and the small forested area that opened up just beyond our yard to a depressed field of tall prairie grasses and wildflowers that extended all the way to the back of the junior high school. I loved that field!

When storms saturated the ground and the 'cricks' overflowed, the Hudson River would back up through the storm catches. The field right beyond our backyard would flood 3-5ft deep and fish from the river swam into the field as it became a makeshift pond! I guess the fish and crayfish were carried by the current, as water spilled and backed up through a network laid down 90 years ago or more. Nor-Easters were definitely my friend growing up, for all the surprising and wonderful things they would bring; days off school, deep puddles and sometimes streets so flooded one needed a canoe to navigate them. I have many wonderful childhood memories of weather. Of course I certainly didn't care for the muskrats that also followed the route of the fishes. They weighed about 15-30 pounds, the size of a medium dog, but had short legs with spiny claws tucked under their bodies. They looked like rats on steroids! They varied in color, but white fur was predominant in the area. Their tails were rat-like and as long as their bodies. Not a favorite critter to say the least!

My bedroom window faced the backyard and field that edged our property. It was a nice place that yellow house. It sat across the street from a Catholic Church and school. Sal's pizzeria was two blocks away, (the same distance from my elementary school) and the junior high, situated behind our property, across the field. We all settled into the house. Mom was a fabulous decorator, eclectic and bold in her tastes. In the living room she placed a large gold chaise lounge; a round leopard print black bamboo rocking chair, with an ottoman in the shape of a big, black mushroom, and a love-seat salvaged and reupholstered from our previous life, and covered the floor with red carpeting. She wallpapered the living room walls in an eclectic, eye-popping zebra-stripe print, separated by silver wallpaper panels. She built a floor to ceiling bookcase, and covered the books in scraps of the silver wallpaper. Mom also enclosed the dining room, which led into the living room by a large arched opening, with plywood and covered the plywood in Gesso. She painted a mural, depicting Romeo and Juliet, surrounded with little vignettes of their lives. She was inspired by a play with Richard Burton she had seen in New York City, and feverishly painted over a month or so! She was a wonderful, dramatic artist. She used the panel she had created to divide the space from the dining room, creating another bedroom, in which a boarder, Andrew, occupied.

She also divided the living room from the front area we called the sun room, into a sitting room and sewing room with modern couches in black and white, separated by black folding shutter partitions, with window shutter to match. The décor was very well done; it was a happy, energetic home. Mothers' bedroom was French provincial, furniture of white and gold lattice, a lady's room. The bedroom I shared with my younger sister, Karen, was done in pink and ruffles; we had a pink carpet and ruffle laced curtains Mom had sewn with bedspreads to match, Oy Veh!

The house Mom rented after the divorce came under the heading of 'haunted'. The spirit seemed to want us to know He was there. Mom said that I complained shortly after moving into the house that, someone stood in the hallway, but wasn't there! Over the next few months, as I got used to the creaks and sounds of the house, I came to notice that around the same time every night, someone would walk down the stairs, each night causing the third step down to make its distinctive squeak. Then the 'someone would walk back up a little while later. Being curious, I wondered if it was Mom or my brother engaging in this nightly ritual. I began to keep my door opened a crack to spy out who it was. My bunk bed, separated from the bottom half, was positioned right next to the door and below the light switch; I could see out, through the door cracked open an inch or so, but could never see anyone by the landing or on the stairs. I wasn't the only family member hearing this. Both Mom and Bruce heard the same thing, thinking it was Karen or me sneaking downstairs in the middle of the night. Secretly, we each individually attempted to ascertain who the culprit was! None of us shared this information of what we heard most nights. Sometimes it would abruptly stop for months, and just when we forgot about it or thought perhaps an active imagination was the cause, or maybe it had just been the sounds of the house settling, it would begin all over again!

During supper one evening, after a particularly noisy night, Bruce complained about the nightly runs keeping him up when he had to get up early for school, turning to me and my sister, accusingly, as the perpetrators. I protested saying, "it wasn't me,' and shared my own experience of hearing the invisible person walking up and down the stairs. That was the beginning of many years of unsettling yet amusing events living with Tony the Ghost.

We found out from the owner of the property we rented, that a cousin, Anthony, and his wife lived in the house for many years, raising their family. It kind of became a mystery when we were told that Tony had fallen from the top of the stairs, and died on the small landing below on the main floor. It was speculated that he may have had a heart attack as he was about to descend the steps and died when striking his head, having tumbled all the way down. Or it was rumored he may have been pushed. We never did find out exactly what had occurred, except for the fact that he died, after having fallen down the stairs dying at the bottom of the landing.

Bruce's room was very small, and had just enough space to accommodate a bed, dresser and night stand. Bruce built shelving for his stereo and books, and was quite cozy. He used the attic stairs as a makeshift drawer, on which he stored his socks and shirts and other clothes and such. As he was getting ready for school one morning, Bruce needed a fresh shirt, and went to open the attic door to his 'drawer'. Just as he opened the door, he saw a face looking at him smiling! It scared the bejeebers out of him; his feet hardly touched the stairs as he ran down like a bolt of lightning into the kitchen!

I had a similar experience a year later. The refrigerator had been going on the fritz. As Bruce tinkered around with it, he asked for a tool. I volunteered to retrieve it from his room. As I rummaged through his toolbox, I found the item and turned around to go back downstairs. As I did, I happened to look up at the attic door, which was open a few inches, and saw a gentle face looking at me smiling! I screamed and ran as fast as I could down the eight foot hallway, grabbed the banister, and launched myself down the stairs! Shaken, I told the family what had happened. This experience was different for me, in that ghosts and spirits, I became aware of them, and acknowledged their presence. Most people, my brother included, chose to file an encounter (non carbon based), in the back of the mind, under the heading, "anomaly", Tony the Ghost just popped up whenever he wanted to, whether he was believed in or not!

Family members weren't the only ones to have moments with Tony. My grandmother Susan was visiting with her friend Emily from Chicago. Emily slept in the sun room on one of the couches. She was a light sleeper. One night she heard someone come down the stairs and go into the kitchen. Having difficulty sleeping, she threw on her robe, thinking she would join my mother for a late night cup of tea. When Emily went into the kitchen, she found it dark and empty, but she knew someone had gone in there. Puzzled, she began to make her way back to the sun room and back to bed. Then, as she got to the stairs, she heard someone going up, and went to the landing to say goodnight, but no one was there, except the squeak of the third step, with no one on it! She quickly made her way back to her bed, and had a very restless and long night.

Tony the Ghost was very protective of 'his' property and I found out the hard way that, if I 'abused' the house, by slamming the door, there were repercussions! He apparently didn't care for cussing either, and would retaliate in some form. He would usually take a personal item from the offending party, and would not return it unless an apology was received. It took years to figure this out!

One day, I was in a particularly bad mood, having had a stressful day at school. Then, coming home, I was chided for not having done my chores. I stomped upstairs to my room and slammed the door as hard as I could. I picked up my hair brush from the vanity and slammed it down, cussing. A book jumped off the shelving above my bed, surprising me. I turned to look, and when I turned back to the vanity to grab the brush, it had disappeared! Strange? Mad, I looked all over the area on my hands and knees, then moving further and further away from the immediate area. The brush was nowhere to be found, as I searched under and over every item in the room. I puzzled over this for a moment, wondering how the brush could just simply disappear. I had an "ah ha" moment, connecting the dots of missing items and my outbursts. Then it suddenly occurred to me that Tony the Ghost was up to his games. I sensed the issue; Anger annoyed Tony!

Realizing I was being disrespectful, I decided to apologize to the house for my actions. I did so, turned around, and the brush was back on the vanity! Very startling. All the members of the family experienced personal items that turned up missing; asking, and, at times, accusing each other of taking stuff without permission. Eventually, I shared my experience with family members and suggested that if something personal were to go missing, they should apologize to the house, and see what happens. It worked most of the time. Interestingly enough, the item usually reappeared shortly after a sincere apology; just saying the words did not affect a return.

One item Tony refused to return to me was a record album. The movie “Helter Skelter”, having just been released, had played over a couple nights on television. I watched it to its conclusion, but it never answered a question that came to mind: In the movie, it was said that Manson was inspired by the Beatles “White Album” song of the same title as the movie, to commit his crimes. Manson said that the song spoke of race riots and how minorities would rise to take over the world with great violence. One day I snuck down to the basement where my brother stored his record collection. He was out on his own at this time. We all respected each others’ personal property, but he wasn’t around to ask so, I went through the collection and ‘borrowed’ his Beatles album, so I could study the song closely, to understand or comprehend what Manson was talking about. I played it over and over, not ‘getting’ what Manson heard? To me, it was a song about a relationship and sex! I blared the music day and night for a couple days. I went to sleep one evening after listening to the album again, over and over, leaving the record on the turntable. When I awoke the next morning, I found the album cover on the radiator, one record left in the jacket. When I looked at it, the album cover appeared strange, warped. I picked it up and pulled the record out of its sleeve to find it was totally warped, as though it was heated up! It was summer, the heat was not on! I had borrowed the album without permission... I went to check out the other album left on the turntable; it was gone. I knew instantly what happened. Tony the Ghost was upset that I had played loud music repeatedly, which I knew bothered him on occasion. I apologized to the house, nothing. Over the course of a couple of weeks I waited for the return of the album, but it never was given back. I had to fess up to my brother that the records were ruined, and told him I would eventually replace it. Being a kid, it would take a while to save up enough from my allowance. Bruce was disappointed, but not really concerned, kind of writing it off and forgiving me.

After a few more years in the house, Mother decided to move to Chicago. On moving day, I resumed my search for the album; I never forgotten that Tony had taken it. I even found the hiding place where Tony stashed things he had not returned, I discovered the stash when I was cleaning the attic stairs and came across a loose floor board on the stairs, and pulled it back, and inside found barrettes, jewelry, silverware, and items of clothing... all sorts of things, but, the album was not there. I guess he had really been mad!

Tony the Ghost protected more than the house though. Mom had recounted times when she was really sick, and she would sense a presence in her room, lovingly watching over her. I experienced the same thing when Mom was in the hospital, having surgery. I was worried about her, and wondering if she was okay. In those days, children were not allowed to visit. As the days passed while Mom was in the hospital, I noticed that in the morning as I made my bed, I would feel a presence standing in the threshold of my bedroom door. Then the next day, the presence turned into a shadow, with the outline of a tall man. Then the next day, there was the figure of a man at the threshold. I knew who it was; it was Tony the Ghost, reassuring me, letting me know he was watching over us. Once I 'got it', he never appeared again, but the sense of comfort and feeling supported never left me. He still cared about us, and would visit on occasion, in times of crisis.

My Mother began exploring religion and spirituality around this time while still on Chamberlain Avenue, and taking palmistry lessons from the renowned Art Nash. She had mentioned some of the incidences that had occurred at the house, and Mr. Nash gave her a ritual to perform should the sightings continue. Mr. Nash explained to Mother that Tony was 'trapped' between worlds, and his soul needed to move on, but required help. So, after a frightening experience, she brought me upstairs to the attic door, and drew a pentagram in salt, and placed a lit white candle in the center of the salt, invoking his presence. Then we said prayers for his soul to move on, into the light, and to those whom loved him. We were never bothered by Tony the Ghost again. I know that the ritual performed helped him cross over.

I didn't know him in life. We found in the basement at one point, his dog-tags. He fought in WWII. As a spirit, he was truly a wonderful friend, even though we didn't understand each others' intentions at the time. I think he tried his best to get his message across, and after some time, we figured it out. I know Tony has found his freedom from this world. In part, asking for release of his soul, and, for him to reach out to those who loved him, awaiting a moment when, he realized there was something more, beyond his ideas, and beyond the yellow Cape Cod house.

Chapter Eleven

Chicago

In 1976, I was a little over twelve years old when we moved to Chicago. I was more than happy to shake my shoes of Little Ferry, being an outcast in a small town; a fresh start in a new place. I knew we were moving before we were told. I had psychically overheard a conversation in which Mom told Grandma Susan that she was not making it, financially. As I played in my room, I spontaneously became aware of intense emotions. Of course, being curious, I allowed the awareness to expand within me, and found my conscious mind listening to my Mother and Grandmother talking over the telephone. Mom couldn't pull in enough income from the jobs she worked, and her last ditch effort of appealing to the state for food and/or housing assistance, anything to help with the bills, was bogged down in red-tape. The support from our Father was extremely meager, and didn't even cover the cost of a pair of sneakers. Grandma said that the first floor apartment had been vacant for a while, and it would be so good to have her near.

I began to feel guilty, and became very upset, feeling like a burden. I left my bedroom and went downstairs, making sure Mom didn't hear me go past as she continued to talk in the bedroom off the kitchen. I continued to the basement, where my favorite rocking chair was. I put my radio headphones over my ears, then rocked and cried. I cried because Mom was in a crisis, and because I didn't want to move! A little while later Mom came down pulled the headphones away from my ears with a look of great concern across her face, and asked why was crying? I didn't think they would be able to hear me, but I had it backwards; I couldn't hear me cry! She calmed me down, and I told her of her and Grandma's plans. She was definitely taken aback, since she had just hung up the phone, and nobody knew except her and Grandma. Mom explained the situation as best she could, or more so, answering my questions from what Grandmothers' end of the conversation I mirrored back. They had come to an agreement that we would move to Chicago, she and the kids, and move into the first floor apartment, which had been vacant for a while. (déjà vu) Mom said it would be a wonderful adventure, and I'd have a new school. Now, that appealed to me!

A few months later we all pitched in, packing our belongings and loaded the truck. Our tiny family caravan consisted of the largest moving truck available, and Mom's car driven behind. Mom and Bruce took turns with driving, but Bruce was definitely more confident and fearless behind the wheel of the truck, with our worldly possessions.

The City of Chicago was quite a different environment; cement and buildings replaced trees! One thing that was not new was my reception to the new home...
We moved in with Grandma Susan; she had a two story flat in the heart of the south-central side of Chicago. Each neighborhood had its own name and flavor. Ours was called 'Little Village'. All the homes were built close together, with fences separating property and domain. Also quite strange and unique were the many houses that sat below the street level. Some buildings were level with the street, with stairs leading to the front door, and others, like ours, were 8-10 feet lower. I couldn't figure out why that was. Later, I found out that most of Chicago was built upon swamp land, and portions of it sank! Also, an extensive network of underground tunnels, sewer systems, and razing of street levels ran throughout the city. Some of the houses were built up; others were recessed as far from the street as possible, creating a front and back yards, while others homes came right up to the sidewalk.

We left the moving truck parked on the street, and just brought our personal belongings in the first night. I took a wonderfully long hot bath, in a tub I could completely submerge in, knees and all. What a luxury. I got ready for bed, said my good nights, and turned in. I crawled into bed beneath a thick, heavy feather tic blanket, needed for the chilly evenings, and against the damp air as the house was situated near Lake Michigan. As I laid down, the table lamp still on, and twisting to turn it off, I observed someone standing at the doorway, but not! I was startled for a moment, then, sensed a large, tall figure standing in the doorway, a vision that entered my mind, but I couldn't 'see' it. It walked over to my bed, sat down, and someone began to stroke my hair, I was stunned to say the least! Staring at the impression pushing the side of the mattress down, I freaked a bit. I yelled at what or whoever it was to go away! Slowly, the gentle and, I felt, the loving stroking of my hair stopped. It got up off the bed, along with the impression on the bed, and walked out of the door.

Welcome to Chicago!

I described my experience in the morning to Mom and Grandma. I told them of what I sensed from the spirit visitation. Even though I couldn't see the spirit itself, I got an impression similar to sight/vision. I felt the presence of a large woman, both tall and heavy and in her late 60's or 70's. Impressions flooded my mind; she liked sweets and wore her hair up, piled on top of her head. She wore a loose roomy drab dress. I described my great grandmother, Victoria, whom I had never met. Mom took it in stride; Grandma Susan seemed totally surprised. I do not recall ever discussing the subject with Grandma.

I wonder if she ever put together that when doors would slam shut with a large resounding bang, it was great grandmother Victoria throwing a temper tantrum every once in a while when she disapproved of something going on in the household? Now that I think of it, it's funny I moved from a house where the ghost held great disdain for slamming doors in anger, and now here, the ghost slammed doors to gain attention!

I would catch great grandma peaking in, her watching or becoming aware, like a veil being lifted or a television turned to a specific station. It was the way she just popped up sometimes, that could be disconcerting. I was called upstairs one afternoon and got a running start from our downstairs living room, ready to bolt up the stairs. As I charged up, focused on the effort, I looked up as I neared a slight curve leading to the landing on the second floor. As I did, great grandma Victoria stood on one of the steps. It was too late; I ran right through her! I was not amused!

Things really didn't get better in Chicago; they just shifted in another way, another direction. Being an adolescent, beginning my teenage life was, in the least, a challenge. I didn't understand the dangers of the city, and was more confined than ever. I couldn't travel far from home nor be out past dusk, which is when life began in the city. Intrinsically, even at that young age, I understood that! I had to stay behind our gate once darkness came. I was not a happy camper, and at a time when rebelliousness emerges in a young person, hormones rage, life could become difficult on everybody. Grandmother always though my music was too loud in the apartment above, and would thump on the floor with a broom. That was my signal to turn it down. I never could turn it down enough, it seemed. These differences drove a wedge between my

Grandmother Susan and me. I grew angry and resentful that I couldn't even enjoy my music under my own roof. School was a nightmare now, as I had to deal with gangs instead of idiots who didn't like me. Life certainly shifted during those years. The visions didn't get any better either. I still saw the plane crashes. Oh, the plane crashes, the worst vision was still yet to come.

Chapter Twelve

Triple Visions

In Chicago, we lived on the same block as ST. Paul's church, a beautiful gothic building built before the Columbian Exposition, by German immigrants. I was intrigued to learn that in its construction, not one metal nail was used; all pieces and masonry interlocked, even the pews. It originally had five steeples, but a terrific fire caused by lightning (if memory serves me correctly) destroyed two of them. The Catholic establishment took up a significant portion of the city block with its church, rectory, nunnery/ convent and school across the street, and other buildings where the priests lived.

I was introduced to St. Paul's, being dragged there for high holidays, and the annual midnight mass on Christmas Eve. Grandma was a devout Catholic, and never missed a service unless illness prevented her. Even through times of thick or thin, she never failed to give tithing, even while living on a very fixed income of $62.00 a month from SSI. Grandma Susan taught china painting, for additional income, having taken up the art years ago. When she could no longer run her beauty shop, she went full time into painting, teaching, entering art shows, and selling her painted china pieces. She was very accomplished in everything she lent her talents to.

I walked passed that church every day, sometimes admiring its architecture, the beautiful brick details, and enormous intricate stained glass windows. I enjoyed admiring the building from either side of the street until I realized one day that I didn't care to walk on the side of the street on which the church was situated. This aroused my curiosity. I sensed an impression, a 'feeling' from the building. It was neither, good nor bad, just a curious unease. I mentioned this to Mom eventually, and asked her what it meant. She recommended I go inside the church and meditate. I didn't really care for this idea, but felt she knew best, and got the gumption a couple of days later to do as she suggested. Around 3pm one afternoon, I went to the massive front doors of St. Paul's and found them open. I went inside quietly, like a stranger in a new land. I observed that the church was dimly lit, as I passed beyond the heavy, ornately carved wooden front doors. There was a huge sculpture of Christ on the cross, his feet highly polished from people touching them, straddled between two more large, massive double doors leading inside the chapel, with a deep marble bowl beneath the statue filled with holy water. Along the walls were Stations of the Cross, all handmade sculptures, small grottos between, and confessional booths. There were large iron candle stands, 8-12 rows deep, holding nine day red glass novena jars. They were placed in front of nearly twice life-sized statues of saints, placed where people could light candles for prayers of loved ones in need, or for the dead, perhaps in purgatory, or simply to remember them. Each candle, a token of thoughts and memories, stood in row after row before a box below it with a slot for donations. Above, facing inward towards parishioners were saints on the pillars spanning throughout the interior of the church, approximately every five pews, hanging above about ten feet. On small shelves, were stature, that were hand carved by craftsmen, that stood a couple of feet tall, they were positioned to relay a message, through a posture or the way it held its arms outstretched, or head looking up or bowed low.

Slowly I made my way deeper inside the chapel. The Altar ahead, surrounded in marble and dark mahogany wood drew my eyes. A platform a few inches high, with a sturdy wood railing separated the space between parishioners' pews and holy land. I allowed my senses to open as I walked up the aisle. I smelled remnants of frankincense and myrrh in the low light from the stained glass windows and candles flickering along the interior walls. It was peaceful, touched with a sense of awe. There was nobody there, not even a priest.

At one point I felt a need to pause and sit. I slid on the hardwood pew, pushing in a few scoots. I looked up and there was a statue of St. Francis suspended above on a shelf. I looked at him casually gazing around, his arms opened, spread wide reaching in the air deep from the shoulders as though he was expecting something, or making a gesture of giving something up to the universe. As I relaxed and looked back at the statue, his arms began to slowly move! Slowly and naturally, both arms gently moved down beside his long robes, hands now facing inside and against his statue body. I closed my eyes in disbelief of what I had just seen. I reluctantly looked again at the statue. The arms were still in the lowered position, but now his head was crooked, looking down instead of up and out. I closed my eyes again, confused and feeling a sensation of weight on my body. I ventured to look once more, to see if his position had really changed. It had; he was still looking down towards me, arms down. I took off as fast as I could, scared and shaken up. I couldn't understand what just happened. I have seen that statue before when, out of respect for Grandma Susan's wishes, I attended church on occasion. How could a statue move?

A week later I went back, to prove to myself that perhaps it had not happened, and my imagination had somehow gone wild. I walked straight up to the place where the statue resided; it remained as I had witnessed it last, looking down with arms down! What did this have to do with the ambiguous feeling of passing by the church? I puzzled over it for a week or so, then, finally confessed to my Mother what had occurred. She suggested meditating on it. I would have preferred an answer straight out, but that didn't happen. So, I followed her advice and meditated on it, seeking answers to the strange visions and occurrences, the ambiguous feelings that I could not discern

as either positive or negative.
I lay upon the gold chaise lounge that was now a part of our new living room. Mom was at work and Grandma at an art show. I had the house to myself; I was free of disturbances. I took slow deep breathes and quieted my thoughts. I understood what meditation was before I was taught, like most everything. There is this place, a moment inside me where I can let go of all earthly concerns. I've found experiences similar to my own, in books I would come across, which confirmed to me that the existence of such experiences were validated, in that, others could explain the sensorial travels. Throughout my life I have found that I initiate research into any subject only after I first experience it, and then validate my experiences by reading stories of others.

I had learned how to allow every muscle, tendon and tissue, every nerve and fiber, to relax and go limp.. After a few more deep breathes, I closed my eyes. At the time, I had a guide. It is intriguing that I only became aware of my guide(s) once I entered a deep calm. I called out from that calm space to her, to lead me on this journey, to seek answers. She came smiling and joyous into that place of inner vision, another realm hidden within. I believe my guide called herself Alicia. We had met in my dreams on and off for as long as could remember. She was beautiful and self-assured, emitting a light from within her. I admired her very much, and she was a loyal friend. I didn't know it at the time, but I later discovered that she was actually me, as an adult! (curiouser and curiouser)

I meditated on the chaise. My guide, Alicia, was alone this time when I called. She warned me that I may want to reconsider seeking information, as we climbed up a precipice. I couldn't understand why? I needed to resolve this issue and the very strange events surrounding my initial unease with passing by the church. I know what I experienced, yet couldn't wrap my mind around it. She agreed to assist me, and all of a sudden picked me up, and tossed me through the air. I then found myself standing in a strange room. Looking around, I tried to figure out where I was. Then, through two large swinging doors a gurney was being pushed by a nurse and doctor. I saw my brother in spirit also watching, but couldn't seem to communicate with him, though he was aware I was there. Turning my attention to the gurney, I watched as my Mother was being wheeled into an operating room for surgery. I became frightened! Why was Bruce there in spirit? I was also worried about the outcome of the procedure. I stood there in this ethereal room, time a sensation, motion ambiguous. Bruce also continued keeping watch, as a shadow, waiting. The doctor emerged from the operating room and said that the operation was successful, and she would fully recover. Bruce then faded out, the room faded out and I faded out, being pulled with great force somewhere else.

I sort of blanked out and 'awoke' at an airport inside the body of a man walking to board a plane. I was fixed inside him, knowing I was somehow tagging along. I was fascinated. I couldn't recall anything like this happening before with a human being. However, I didn't question it much, and went along with the experience. There was a sensation of being suspended, a flow of consciousness, however, the feeling of being caught in an energy that grabbed me, and I could not resist but be pulled by this invisible force.

In the vision, the plane was crowded, but the man easily made his way to his seat, put his briefcase in the overhead storage bin, and sat in the seat nearest the window. He seemed like a nice guy, and was happy he was returning home to his family. I could 'hear' the thoughts of others all around me, chattering away; it was a bit overwhelming, but very interesting too. The seatbelt and smoking sign came on, and the stewardess did her spiel on where things on the plane were located, what to do in an emergency, and where the emergency doors were located. A baby cried throughout the presentation. The man I was stuck to fastened his seatbelt, anxious to get on his way. The plane taxied down and smoothly lifted off the ground. A moment, maybe two, passed; then there was a shutter, then another. He grabbed the arms of his seat and then we were falling! The seat violently moved forward and up, throwing him into the seat in front. He was immediately decapitated! I separated from his body, watching with absolute horror as other people died cruelly. The baby in the arms of the mother smashed up against her, they mushed together on the seat in front of them, and on and on until we hit the ground and exploded. At that point, I fell hard, really hard, back into my body in terrific pain. I was jerked out of the meditation and doubled over, my stomach physically bruised!

I was so upset; it took me days to calm down. I innately understood that this was a vision of events yet to occur. I didn't know what to do. Who do I tell, who do I warn of this impending disaster? I just didn't know. And I didn't try to communicate this vision to anybody in authority. I only told my Mother. I also asked if she was sick. She said she was having stomach issues, and was preparing to see her doctor about it. A few months later, Mom did have surgery to remove her gallbladder, and it was successful.

Shortly following, to my great, great dismay, the airplane crash occurred in Chicago. It was 1977.

I found out I wasn't the only one to have had a knowledge/vision of the incident, and was glad to learn others did try to warn authorities. I still carry a large amount of shame I didn't reach out. Maybe one more person calling authorities might have made the difference? I will never know.

I asked my guide, Alicia, on several occasions who she is, and why she is always available to me when I close my eyes and call? For a long time, she would not answer these questions. There was even an older woman, deep into her 90's who sometimes accompanied her. This woman/spirit was potent, powerful and so gentle and wise; she is hard to truly explain. She helped Alicia when I posed a question she didn't know how to answer, or when my life became complicated. The old woman's presence had a soothing quality, and I was able to believe and know everything would work out alright.

During one meditation session, it occurred to me that I did not need an answer from Alicia; I could psych it out myself! So this is what I endeavored to do. It took all of the abilities I had learned and mastered at the time, and I was finally successful! How can one explain scattered mosaics of moments and memories littering time? This is the closest I can come, to explain or relationship(s):

...With my body deeply relaxed, so much so that I do not know where I begin or end, being aware of my physical body, but numb to sensation, I turned my vision within. I moved through layers that are like places or initiative stepping stones, this is quite difficult to explain... Each stepping stone is a level, moving or propelling my consciousness beyond my body, and aspects of ego; it has dimensions which change as you travel further onward. These dimensions have a, a substance; richer than the waking, everyday third dimension we primarily live in. If you are not careful, the delicious, inviting elements that exist can steal you away. One moment you are enjoying a breeze, and all of a sudden you are the breeze moving over and through the world! You have to learn to be aware, yet not become involved.

One time I journeyed to a place Alicia would take me when we prepared to travel. It was very much like a craggy precipice, or the edge of a cliff. She would ask me to hold my intention firmly in my mind; the intention would create direction, and bring us to the place or information sought. Then came a leap; a 'leap of faith' off the precipice and fly, allowing the buoyancy of the air to support us. I went to our meeting place and approached the edge of the peak. Looking out over the landscape, there was mountain after mountain which shifted shapes, as I surveyed as far as I could see. As I focused on a spot, it sometimes 'shifted' and became a story, as if watching a movie but real, not unlike a 3D IMAX theater experience.

Again, this place is tricky, and if you tarry too long you might find yourself involved in the event. I was careful to maintain my focus and intention of finding out who is Alicia? I felt myself begin to lift and becoming light, as a feather... This little adventure was different from others I had had before in that, when I began to travel, I was aware that a part of me, my consciousness, was still paused at the edge of the cliff. Interesting! I seemed to move through time, time, time... moving through moments together, alliances and instances where she assisted me when I was unaware. Time was moving as memory and sensation; emotions were changing like scenes along the course of a play. Then time somehow condensed, and Alicia and I began to merge. Our essences actually merged as we became one being! I could see this as though I were looking into a mirror, Alicia now emanating from my eyes. I was stunned, flabbergasted, amazed and confused. How can she be me? An answer came as soon as the thought was formed, and it said she is a portion of your soul, that which cannot be contained. When I learned the secret, that Alicia and I were one and the same, she and the older woman came into my internal vision, smiling and laughing. Alicia said I wouldn't have believed her if she had told me; I had to discover it for myself. She asked if I had discovered the other secret. I looked at her a long and hard, then at the old woman, and I knew. She was also me, but far older! I have not yet come across anyone else who has had this experience of being their own guide, at different intersections in time, spiritual development, and spanned across the event of a single lifetime. I have read and heard of others being guided by a previous life personality, but then again, if I think about it, it's very similar, yet this thus far, is unique to my knowledge.

Chapter Thirteen

Thunder and Rain

A new life in the city of Chicago was an experience totally exhilarating and foreign for me. I had limits on my freedom never before imposed; getting along with Grandma Susan, and being a teenager was enough to deal with, but more layers had been added.

I could feel energetically the internal angst and difficulties Mother faced working long, hard hours at one or two jobs. We have always had a strong connection and, besides my own feelings, I inadvertently picked up on hers, like living two lives at once! It took a while before I learned the difference between what I was feeling personally, and, what was the result of connecting or 'plugging' into the turmoil of others I cared about. Beyond being a loving daughter, psychically, I also felt the emotions of those close to me. I had to learn to differentiate between what "I" was feeling as I moved through life, but also identify the feelings of others. Through research into my experiences, I discovered I am also an empathic.

I was a frustrated young person, which translated

into light bulbs not working, electronics going nuts. I occasionally practiced psychokinesis, successfully moving the hands of a clock that hung on the wall above the chaise lounge. Then I made a new discovery of something I could do; I could create thunder storms. I may sound farfetched. However, I can only state my experiences, observations and conclusions. Yet, as I experimented, replicated and had results, validated by experiences from witnesses at the time, I can only report this next leap in understanding of the human potential to effect environment.

It has been found that when a young adolescent person is troubled in a household, the effects can be poltergeist in nature. Most poltergeist experiences are usually directly correlated to a youth with emotional issues. Poltergeists are associated with things breaking, items of their own accord flying across a room, and destructive, frightening episodes experienced by all members of the family. The perpetrator is usually thought to be an unruly ghost, but the actual 'ghosts are built up emotions psychically expressed. It is not intentional. The individual in the family from which these powerful psychokinetic forces originate, are not aware that they are the culprit. Most of these strange experiences are filed in the family skeleton closet, and forgotten by most once the 'poltergeist' stops. I mention this again because I believe, in a way that I learned how to direct or perhaps harness these powerful emotional forces. I made the connection of my foul moods and the incidence of electronics failing. This led me to investigate psychokinesis, and the power of the human mind. The results are something I shall never forget and through them I learned that there are some things better left to Nature.

I watched a program on television as a young teenager that explained how it was believed that the atmosphere, stratosphere, ionosphere and such collaborated to create weather. The program primarily focused on how thunder, lightning and rain developed. Near the same time, I had heard about people dissipating clouds by throwing thought-energy, i.e., imagining the cloud simply disappearing from the sky. Housewives did it folding their families' laundry in the backyard.

I tinkered and began to experiment with the idea of dissipating clouds. First, I imagined, within the confines of my mind, observing clouds, trying to make them disappear. No luck. Then I stood outside and focused on a specific cloud. A rule of physics says that; when one focuses energy of thought (an intention) and belief (confidence), dynamics merge, thus making the desire, so. However, I found myself attached to the clouds and enjoyed them; so billowy, towering atop the other, building and growing higher and higher, so bright, an island-like topography developing in the sky. The clouds made shadows, canyons and peaks not unlike a sandcastle on a summers' day along the seashore. The clouds I was concentrating on grew instead of dissipate! This was going in the wrong direction!

I sought information during one of my meditations, inquisitive as to why I couldn't make the clouds disappear. I projected the question, which means, I sent what I call an energetic message, and waited for a source to echo an answer back...

...An image filled my mind like a camera aperture opening from a narrow, singular field of vision, and enlarging to a wide angle. I saw in my mind the different 'spheres' reacting along one another. I played a game, becoming involved; I imagined moisture rising up into the sky, creating clouds, then those clouds bumping up against each other, winds coming down from high above at a 45 degree angle, icy, cold down through warm convection breezes, then circulating into a spiral type motion, without completing a full rotation, and moving creating lightning. That was my answer; not what I expected!

I used this information as I attempted to master techniques of creating clouds instead of un-creating them. I found that I enjoyed clouds, loved and revered them. I truly did not want them to disappear. I changed strategies: Experimenting within my imagination, I would pick an area where I wanted weather to begin, and focused all of my attentions, throwing my anger, perhaps angst into the equation, which represented energy. I found out this was not a good thing to do, but it worked!

I was again having issues with Grandma Susan. Mom was not sure what to do. She was between her teenage daughter and her elderly Mother. One dreadful day, I was sitting in my favorite rocking chair in the living room after Mom left for work. I was angry that I was not able to turn on the stereo, as instructed by Mom after further complaints from Grandma. No matter how low I set the volume, shortly after turning on the stereo a "thump, thump, thump!" pounded above me from the ceiling. Grandma, with a broomstick in hand, would pound on the floor, telling me to turn it down. I sat back in a favorite chair, rocking gently, attempted to calm myself and looking out of the windows, to the street above. I had a whole evening alone, without music and escape ahead of me. I was confined to the house, because the city was such a dangerous place, I was told (truly clueless). I sat and meditated, moving my attentions to imagining gathering clouds. Not much time had passed when the skies darkened; a brilliant fall afternoon became ominous and foreboding. Lightning ripped through the sky and the winds picked up, blowing hard and furiously. I opened my eyes to watch lightning move through the sky, and then concentrated on a spot where I wanted to see a lightning bolt. After about three minutes, it streaked through the clouds! Woof! I decided to bring the storm a little closer, focusing on drawing the winds in my direction, to where I sat near the living room windows. Then suddenly, a single bolt of lightning struck in the middle of the street, in front of the house! I sat transfixed, my eyes glued to the spot the lightning had hit, as wisps of smoke rose in the air. This instantly brought me out of my angry state, the product which was directed at the house and my Grandmother. I knew there was a connection, yet, failed to believe it. I felt guilty, though, and afraid that I might have caused her harm. The lightning strike was that close; the coincidence, mindboggling.

At that moment, I flashed back to being a young girl, walking to school... Ahead of me was an old woman. A thought occurred to me that she would trip and fall. No sooner did I think this that it actually occurred! I was shocked, and then felt guilty and puzzled. Did I cause her to fall by thinking it? Or, did I 'pick up' that she was going to fall?

It took repeated experiments, over a couple of years, watching the news for a conducive weather forecast, then, making plans or, intentions of creating the lightning I adored so much. Forecasts had to be clear of any variances or possibilities of generating storms within a few hundred miles. I discovered it took me 40 minutes to whip something up. Now, this one I never figured out; if a storm was brewing, as I looked into the sky, I would 'know' where a thunderbolt would appear. A thunderbolt of a brilliant flash, white hot lightning and a sonic-like rumbling boom! I also projected thoughts that a bolt of lightning would occur at a specific point in the air. Then, after about three minutes, it would appear.

I showed many friends, but they either thought it a coincidence, or had absolutely nothing to say. They'd just walk away and shake their heads. Sometimes I wouldn't see those friends for a while (I guess) until the event faded from their memories, or it was simply blown off as just plain weird, filed away in the, "I don't know" file in their brains!

After many seasons of experimenting, I thought I had it down pretty well. One evening, I went on a date. A lovely storm was brewing in the distance, outside the city, over Lake Michigan. I met him at his place, and he wanted me to come upstairs for a minute before we left. I wasn't very comfortable with this idea, but agreed for just a moment to see his place. He was an artist, and wanted to show me a few pieces. His work was on large canvasses. His brushstrokes were bold, harsh in oils, with strong religious overtones. We talked for a short time as I stood close to the door I had left opened, and commented on one of the paintings with lightning and thunderbolts as the one that most appealed to me. Then, being young and somewhat ignorant, I said, "You know, I have a special talent with lightning," and mentioned some examples of my energetic experiments. He said, "You're joking." I said, "I am quite serious," feeling mocked. Wanting to get on with our date, I suggested we leave. We went downstairs to the parking lot. I said, "I'll prove what I stated is true." I then instructed him to look at a certain spot in the sky; I concentrated for a moment, then pointed, and said, "Look where I am pointing." He followed my outstretched hand, and then at that moment, a bolt of lightning came out of a cloud, with a near sonic boom! He stared for a long time in the sky. He then said, "That was a weird coincidence!" Completely blowing the event off and we began our date. (There was that intriguing ability I have seen so many times, to dismiss direct experience.)

We had a wonderful dinner and casual conversation, and then went to a lounge for a few drinks. After he loosened up a bit, he brought up the lightning incident, saying how weird that was. I protested, and said, "It wasn't luck, but something I learned how to do after a lot of practice," feeling angry. He still didn't believe me, for which I do not fault him, but, he got a bit nasty after a while. Finally he challenged me to prove to him it wasn't just happenstance. He also started telling others around the bar of my mysterious talent, somewhat embarrassing me. I accepted the challenge. I told him to look at his watch, and in three minutes he would have his proof! I closed my eyes, and in my imagination, I pretended my vision rose to the ceiling, and then beyond to the roof and floated above the building. I imagined the clouds circulating and swirling in a concentrated area above. I sent energy as though my thoughts were a laser beam, feeding heat into the cold layers upon layers of clouds. I opened my eyes, grabbed my drink, and waited. All of a sudden there was a loud "boom" that rattled the glasses hanging above the bar, rattled the windows around the room, and scared everyone within the lounge as people gasped. Then the lights went out! The bartender lit candles and placed them every few feet around the bar. I looked over at my date, which was visibly shaken, leaning far in his chair away from me. I was as wide eyed as he, never expecting something like that to happen! Some of the patrons at the bar who were aware of the bet actually got up and moved to the other side of the large oval bar; some left entirely. Shortly afterward, gathering himself, he suggested we leave. We drove back to his place. He parked the car and without a word, opened his door and left, without even saying goodbye! He just left me sitting there, alone in the parking lot inside his car. I followed him up after a long moment, and walked up the stairs to his flat. He turned, seeing me standing in the doorway. I told him I was worried if he was okay? He didn't speak a word, just carefully stared in my direction. I apologized for scaring him. He found his tongue and began cursing me, saying I was bad or possibly possessed! I needed to embrace the lord and renounce my sins! He was angry, and afraid of me. I tried to explain, but he kept backing away from me, and then screamed at me to leave! I did, scared and confused, running down the stairs to my car, locking the door as soon as I got inside. I thought he might be chasing me! But he hadn't been.

I didn't learn the lesson of keeping my mouth shut very well. I thought that if I proved my contention to my friends, it would appear cool. It was never the reaction!

I moved out to Arizona for a few years in the early 1980's. I met through a neighbor, a man named Jeff. After hanging out for a few weeks, we became a couple. I eventually moved-in with him in his small hometown of Globe, Arizona. There was nothing much there; it was a mining town on the verge of collapsing. I had gotten a job as a chef. Jeff was an apprentice architect.

One day, as Jeff and I sat on his enclosed screen porch, watching clouds form over the foothills, I told him of this strange ability of creating lightning I had learned, which, of course he did not accept. Over the course of time, I endeavored to prove it to him. We would watch the weather forecasts. In the desert, rain can be sparse, even during monsoon season, which generally started in June, and ran through August or September. When I created lightning, nine times out of ten, it was accompanied by rain, though it was not my primary intention. After clear skies had been forecasted for at least a week, which was pretty common, the experiments commenced! I wanted to prove to Jeff, but the experimenting was also my own personal test. Even though I had years of evidence under my belt, I still had lingering doubts. I didn't doubt myself though, while I performed a ritual imaginary practice. Creating weather was different in Arizona than in Chicago. In Chicago, I would mostly call clouds from surrounding areas, even if they were hundreds of miles away. Using the upper air level jet-stream, its fast currents indicative of the area, between the southern flow of moist air, pushing North, and the cold Canadian/Siberian dry air dipping down, cloud creating or calling was not an issue! I would imagine the clouds coming from a couple of directions, and beginning to bump into one another. The higher, colder clouds would dive and penetrate into the warmer clouds closer to the ground and, the result was thunder and lightning. In Arizona, by contrast, there were no clouds to call, or they were too far away to affect a storm on the same day. Plus, I discovered as I worked on technique, that the jet-stream that used to be my friend and helper now thwarted efforts. The jet-stream tends to skirt, to maintain a vast area, a bubble, of high pressure over the southwestern United States, keeping storms from the Pacific Ocean, to the West, flowing East across the U.S., and pushing the Southerly flow, up from Mexico, to the South, as air flows towards Texas and New Mexico. I figured out that I needed to create clouds. I could still project my mind out of my body, and fly over the surrounding area, checking out the terrains and sources of water, and I noticed I could sense water-tables beneath the desert floor, and inside the mountains and mesas. I imagined moisture rising from the ground, from the hills, and from underground waters in a concentrated area. Then I envisioned the moisture rising, and then gathering, condensing to create clouds that reached high in the sky. They had to be a temperature variance. I required cold air masses and clouds high, and then, coming down at an angle, with warmer clouds below to bump into. Once I figured out how to conjure clouds in the desert, I was able to prove my contention to Jeff. After several storms, he uneasily accepted it, still confused by the 'coincidence' of my predictions that on this day, at this hour, we would have a nice storm. It wasn't until one particular day, as time went on, perhaps a month, I realized he really did believe me. Jeff sneaked out of the house one afternoon while I was sleeping. I wondered where he was after waking up, alone. I scanned psychically, attempting to locate him.

I found him, using a technique called, "remote viewing." My consciousness would expand outward, like radar sweeping across an area, radiating. Then a strange juxtaposition occurred, where I would feel passively aware of my physical body relaxing in the chair, and actively aware that, my consciousness is actively moving across the landscape, energetically attracted to my target. I hovered over an area in the foothills, his friends' pick-up truck parked on the top of a mesa. He was drinking with a couple of friends and a girl I knew who was fascinated by him. I was angered by this, having not been invited, and letting her hang all over him, and I set out to ruin their little party. I focused and concentrated on sending a bolt of lightning near where they were. Sure enough, a good storm brewed up after a short time. The sound of the rain comforted me and I let go. After an hour or so, my boyfriend came in, soaking wet, eyes wide and angry! He screamed at me and said, "You nearly killed me and my friends!" I said, "What the hell are you talking about?" He said, "It was a beautiful day, and we were partying in the foothills. The sky grew dark, and before we could react, a bolt of lightning struck right in front of the pick-up truck!" I apologized and said, "It wasn't my intention of harming anyone, I was pissed you left me behind."

Things were never the same from that day forward.

He reacted like everyone else; scared, unable to digest it or, thinking I was somehow possessed by a negative force, or was evil.

I moved back to Chicago not too long after living with Jeff, about nine months' total. It was not by choice, though.

The recession was going strong, especially in the Southwest, and I couldn't find a job to save my soul! Everyone fell on hard times. Jeff lost his position, due to cut-backs. I lost my chef's job after attempting to start a union for the underpaid staff. Not a good move in a small town! I was black-listed.

With lots of time on my hands, I spent the days sitting in my favorite grave yard that had markers from the early 1800's. Some graves were above ground. The cement boxes were about 4 foot high, old, and weather-worn. The older ones were in the earth, sectioned off by a large iron arch, with the name, "AHA" scrolled in rusted metal. There was a lot of 'activity' in this cemetery. I would kick back atop a sarcophagus, leaning against the gate, and watch...shadows. This place had layer upon layer of energies. I sensed that before it was a cemetery, it was a home to a small Native American village. Then, many children died. I felt they were buried in unmarked graves on the property, and then the land was taken over and used as the town graveyard.

It was rare when I felt unwelcomed on the grounds, but the few times the sensation did occur, I was out of there! I suppose with spirits, as with people that, at times they enjoy company, and at other times 'feel' intruded upon, as if by uninvited guests. Also during these days, I would wander and search the foothills of Tonto National Forest for turquoise or quartz and rose quartz to sell. Mostly, I ended up collecting aluminum cans to trade for cash at the local recycler. We lived on "souper rice" in those days; a box of instant rice and a can of condensed soup cooked together and, poof!, a filling meal. Fortunately, we had a friend that worked at the grocery store who would punch on the cash register an item for only a few pennies. She was great. Occasionally, we could buy meat for a quarter. We didn't abuse this gracious gift, though, and I was able to exchange cleaning her house for the food.

There was a period in my life of about seven years during which I could create storms. I learned that messing with the natural course of weather was precarious. Some people learned how to disperse clouds by sending energy to them. I learned, perhaps, the opposite; how to create clouds and then move them. I found out during this time in life that there were massive amounts of people attempting to do the same thing, but trying to send rain to Ethiopia, during those terribly devastating drought years, millions died of starvation. I, too, lent energy at one point. But, it didn't just finally rain, torrential waves of storms saturated the earth, and still no crops would grow, but floods would occur, killing anything growing. Or, the earth was so dry and hard that floods occurred as the water simply stayed on the surface, not soaking into the earth most times. It seemed to me at the time a cruel irony. I puzzled over the situation for years. When California also had a drought phase, again rain was called by many people, and when it came, a similar effect; waves and waves of flooding and mud slides. New problems were created. It was the last time I ever participated energetically in creating weather. I still truly question if, indeed, on an individual and mass basis, we affected the environment, on an energetic level, even though I have seen some amazing things!

Why didn't the intention of creating rain to a drought stricken area also include the ground absorbing the life -giving waters?

I attended a conference in Kentucky, in the mid to late 1980's, and met a man named Serge King. He is a Kahuna, a Hawaiian medicine man. I learned from him that his particular tribe of people were purported to create weather, particularly thunder storms. At least I had a reference, a validation! I didn't believe I was misinterpreting or crazy! Many cultures have their 'medicine men', who ask their guardians, deities, angels or higher source for the gift of life sustaining waters. There are rain dances with great rituals. I suppose I went about my experimenting with creating weather in a western way; learning first of the nature of weather, as much as was known at the time, and then used the 'ritual' of aligning certain energies to affect my environment. Eight out of ten times I was successful in achieving my desire for a storm. The best method however I have ever come across is the American rain dance; wash your car!

Chapter fourteen

1980

1980 was not a good year for my family. My Mother had traveled from Chicago to New Jersey for a visit with my brother, Bruce. She has always wanted to move back, having never being comfortable with the separation of family. Bruce had chosen not to live in Chicago. He had helped us drive out in the moving truck, but left once we were settled. That broke Mom's heart. Though he was only nineteen years old at the time, he was far older than his actual mortal years: An old soul. I know Bruce also missed the family being together, and called me one evening during Mom's visit and asked, "Would you be interested in moving back?" I said, "Not in your wildest nightmares would I consider such a thing! I am in a big city, with lots to do, and I have a boyfriend." He said, trying to convince me, "everything would work out," I said, "Plus, I'm not the town witch here, just another face in the crowd." He said, "We don't have to live in the same town." I ended this long conversation by saying, "I will not change my mind," and refused to hear any more about it.

I wish, I wish I recognized the desperation and loneliness in his voice, from being on his own the last two years. I have been haunted by that conversation ever since.

Bruce had a beautiful girlfriend, Moe. They had been sweethearts since high school. He wanted to marry her, and start his own family. He was deeply in love. She broke up with him a year after we moved to Chicago, saying she needed to spread her wings, and see what the world was about. She was considering going to college in Florida. Moe wasn't ready to settle down and have babies. She loved Bruce very much, but she needed to follow her heart and taste and desires in life. Bruce did his best to get his life together, after such a great blow, and threw his energies into work. As hard as he tried, life spun out of control. For just a singular moment, he lost control, and then lost his life, while Mother was still visiting.

I was back in Chicago getting ready to go out and hang out with a girlfriend, Vida. It was a stormy evening, to my great delight, but, I asked the rain to wait until I reached her house two blocks away. It did! We listened to music from a new album by the band, Boston, and then decided to play cards. Vida gathered munchies for us as we migrated into the kitchen. As she placed the snacks on the table, she gasped, looking at my face as I began to shake uncontrollably, turned pale and jumped up from the table, bolting from the kitchen, into the living room. I felt like I was hit hard in the stomach and doubled over. Vida ran in after me and asked, “What is the problem?” I said, “Someone close to me just died.” I was having problems breathing, like I had been running hard and stopped abruptly and tried to catch my breath. I began to feel lightheaded and paced around the room as Vida stared at me hard, trying to comfort me. I was having trouble focusing, as my mind raced. She encouraged me back into the kitchen, trying to change the subject and get me to eat something. I felt like I was an empty shell, like something important had left me, my body or spirit. Vida watched me closely, frightened as my body became cold to the touch, and even more pale. This went on for 30 or 40 minutes. I tried to get a hold of myself. I had no other information except for the profound feeling of loss. Before she could continue asking me questions, the phone rang, scaring us both! She answered it and came back, saying it was for me, surprised. It was my Father. He said I needed to get home right away. I was confused, still trembling out of control. He told me to sit down. I told him I did, lying, still standing beside the mantle in Vida’s living room. Then he blurted it out, “Your brother Bruce died and you need to go home and tell Grandma, and get out to New Jersey right away.” I dropped the phone and went into shock and panic all at the same time. Vida handed the phone back to me, knowing something was very wrong!

Finding my voice, I said goodbye to my Father and told him we would call when we were on our way. Vida asked me what had happened as she walked me home. I told her, and asked her to watch my animals while I was out of town. She agreed, I gave her my keys to the house, and went inside.

I wandered into a dark house, dazed. My boyfriend Joe had stayed at the house. He heard me come in, and ran from the back of the house towards me, his eyes wide with fright. I asked, "What is the matter?!" He said, "I was taking a bath when the lights started to blink on and off wildly. Then, I heard this animal like guttural shriek, a scream that expressed the depth of pain, and then a shadowy figure passed outside the bathroom door! I thought it was an intruder and I jumped out of the bath water and went to confront whoever it was, still naked, dripping wet, but I couldn't find any one there. I turned around to fetch my clothes and a shadow stood there, towering over me!" Joe said he could see right through it, and felt a great, dark anger and pain somehow emanating from it. This scared the hell out of him. The exaggerated moment seemed to last forever; then the light all blew up! Every light bulb exploded from every fixture within the house, showering him with shards of glass. Joe was ready to bolt from the house, but I was able to calm him down, and told him what happened. The news waylaid his being scared silly and he stood by my side.

I now had the task of going upstairs to tell Grandma, I am seventeen years old. It was late, but, she was usually up, so I climbed the stairs up to her apartment above and knocked on the door softly. She didn't respond, so, reluctantly, I opened the door. Grandma Susan's bedroom was a few steps away, and it was dark. Knowing the short trek, I made my way to the kitchen light switch and stood for a long, long moment before flipping it on. I stepped inside her bedroom, reaching for the bedside lamp. Grandma was tucked deep under a thick feather tic quilt. I gently woke her up. She sat up; surprised, knowing I would never bother her, as I tended to avoid her as much as possible. I moved a little closer into her line of vision, and sat at the edge of her bed, saying I could only recant what had occurred. I told her that her grandson was dead, and we needed to get to New Jersey right away. As soon as the words left my lips, she began to cry and sobbed deeply. I had never seen her cry before, and I witnessed her heart break right in front of me. I did my best to comfort her, and sat with her for a while. Eventually gathering herself together, Grandma Susan said she wasn't up to driving (having a heart condition) and refused to let me drive. I was seventeen, and didn't have a license. Then Joe eventually appearing just inside the kitchen door spoke up, and offered to drive us to New Jersey. We packed a few bags, and got in Grandma's green 1972 Cadillac and headed East, arriving later the next morning, driving straight for about 12 hours.

I walked into my Father's house; mother sat on the porch, in shock. I did what I could with arranging the wake and funeral, but Moe did the most. She was right there and never left my Mother's side. Mom was completely numb through the whole ordeal. There were a few strange twists with my brothers' remains. During the wake, friends had left tokens and mementos in his casket. The night before the funeral, someone had taken these items. We were called into the funeral directors office hours before the service. It was almost too much to emotionally take! The funeral director was beside himself. We found out later that a former lover, who was a Wiccan, broke into the funeral home and stole the items. We never knew the reason why. She began to induct Bruce into the religion, but something inside him did not care for her ideas or practices, more on the 'black' or dark side of the ancient religion. She still wanted a piece of him, perhaps to try and bind his spirit to her, who knows. She was barred from the services and never heard from again.

The only time I cried was when I was butting heads with my Father. I stood at the casket, trying to comprehend my brother lying there. His pose not natural for him, if he was supposed to be portraying sleep. They had placed his hands over his belly, when he had always slept with them across over his chest. My Father came up to me and told me to step aside, so other people could go up and pay their respects. The way he said it struck me the wrong way, and I became enraged! Distraught, I ran downstairs to the restroom lounge, and cried for a few minutes before calming down. Moe was also there, overwhelmed. She offered me comfort and mutual respect. I felt a distinct sense of being near the center of attention; it was quite uncomfortable. Apparently, I was not acting as expected.

It would take ten years before I started the grieving process. There were comments about the lack of tears

I shed at the wake. People were puzzled over it, and whispered of it at the funeral and long afterwards. I found out later that children grieve differently. It may take years, and even decades for grief to arise. Plus, I would be busy dealing with keeping my Mother sane for a great many years to follow.

A few days after the wake and funeral, a select group of Bruce's friends, my Mother and I met at his apartment. Sugar, a dear friend of Bruce's was to lead a séance. I had never attended one before. I went to support Mom. She needed to know he was okay. We sat in a circle in his bedroom, where he had died, and lit a white candle in the center of those gathered. A prayer was lead, and we all clasped hands. Sugar meditated, and put herself into a trance, trying to reach out to Bruce. To my surprise, I followed where her inner vision went, then I followed her out of her body, arriving at a shoreline in the woods. It was misty and thick with a heavy brooding atmosphere. As we became accustomed to our surroundings, hovering above the ground, we looked out over the water, and saw a little boat. Somehow, we were then beside the boat, a man sat in it, head bowed low, with a paper bag over his head. Then we realized it was Bruce! Sugar asked why he had the bag over his head? He said, he was so ashamed, so ashamed he had caused so much pain. Sugar consoled him, and told him it would be okay, that, she and Moe were taking care of Mom. Something happened, and I snapped back to my body, Sugar still there talking to him. I opened my eyes to see others staring at me. After a short time, Sugar came back, and shared the conversation, letting everyone know that he was alright, and there were guides by his side, ready to help him out through his transition. The evening came to a close, and we all went our separate ways, silently. As time passed slowly, different members of the family received messages from Bruce, that he was okay and on the mend. Not all of the messages were understood at first, but they were potent enough to garner serious attention, and invited marvel, at the wonders of the universe and that the forces of love, transcend death.

My Father is a pragmatic person. He was a carpenter and businessman all of his adult life. He never really believed in the spiritual realm, I do not believe he is even religious. He was driving late one night, the road near deserted. He noticed a light in his rearview mirror glowing in red. He saw the number, "19" was illuminated on his back window, surrounded by a glowing square frame around the number. There were no other cars from either direction or, thinking he was seeing things or an odd reflection from somewhere, continued on his way. Still, the number '19' continued to glow brightly. He turned around to see where this could be coming from, and saw nothing but the glowing number. He stopped his car at the side of the road, unnerved by this strange occurrence. The radio too was acting strange; static was blaring out. Slowly, the bright "19" began to fade away. My Father's attentions riveted on the phenomenon! Innately there was a sense that this meant something. All day, actually, the number "19´popped up, Dad mentions: "I'm reading the newspaper comics, and he came across the Peanuts column, and he had 19 nuts prominently in the cartoon story. He saw 19 on license plates." Dad didn't believe or even conceive of after-death communications, but somewhere inside, he knew they were from Bruce; and a peace washed over him unlike anything he had ever experienced before.

Moe had an experience one evening as she relaxed after a trying day. She poured herself a glass of wine, and flipped through radio stations for something interesting. She tuned onto a talk show on the subject of reincarnation. This piqued her interest, and she kicked back, listening and unwinding. The host had a monotone voice, and soon his cadence and drone, and the effects of the wine lulled her into a quiet space, closing her eyes. She was suddenly jarred upright in her chair with a voice shouting out from the radio saying, "Are you not listening? I worked for Checker Cab in New York!" It was Bruce.

On several other occasions, Bruce attempted to establish contact from wherever he was, or try to control certain situations. Ren, Bruces' roommate remained in their apartment alone after Bruce passed away, but Ren couldn't afford the rent on his own so, he decided to search for someone to rent Bruce's former room. A nice young woman answered his advertisement and after looking at the apartment agreed to rent the room. It was a lovely apartment, very spacious and modern. It was an elegantly remodeled mid-century apartment, large windows nearly from floor to ceiling. Intricate coved moldings throughout the apartment, and, hand-crafted windows with deep sills, that was at branch level with broad leafed trees. It created an aesthetically pleasing private sanctuary. Hardwood flooring, plaster and lathe walls with the character of old world craftsmanship yet modern, open and airy. It was clean and contemporary, high ceilings with radiant heat and air-conditioned. Nice. Ren had the loft; the other bedroom was on the main living level.

Once the woman agreed to move in, she asked if she could put on a fresh coat of paint, since Bruce had written limericks and poetry on the walls. It was lovely stuff, but she wanted to make the space her own. Ren said, "Fine." So she commenced to paint the walls in a cheery color that suited her. She spent the better part of a Saturday painting and trimming. The new roommate went about her business, preparing to move all her personal items a few days later after the paint was dry and the room aired out. Opening the bedroom door with bags in hand, she walked into the same room she had just painted over. The new paint had disappeared, and the old color and writings on the wall reappeared! She thought that was odd. She thought the problem was that she had not used a primer, and decided to paint the walls again. She got fresh paint and a heavy duty primer, then, spent the day painting with a girlfriend she had enlisted to help. She came back the next day, and found that the room again had reverted back to the original room; the writing back on the walls. She left and never came back.

FAVORITE TREE

ROMEO + JULIETTE IN HOUSE ON CHAMBERLAIN

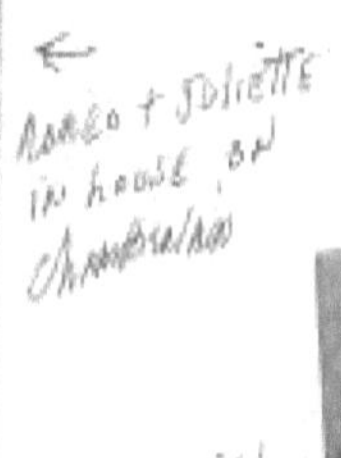

Fish!

Scottie

FIELD BEHIND HOUSE THAT FLOODS

BRUCE KAREN (ME) KATE

My mother Yvonne w/her mother Susan →

↑ Yvonne as child

↘ How houses are @ street level

Ours below ↙

← me

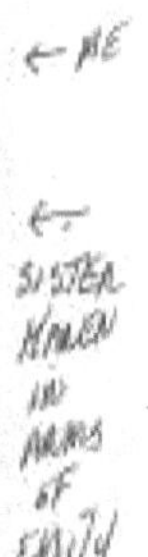

↑ Emily

↑ Chicago house back yard + typical size of yards

GRAND MA SUSAN →

w/ SOME of her ART (china)

GREAT GRANDMA VICTORIA

THE HOUSE IN CHICAGO AFTER RETURN

Chapter Fifteen

Love and Loss

Back in Chicago, things went from bad to worse. Grandma Susan did not emotionally recover from the shock of losing her only grandson, and was hospitalized soon after arriving back into town. She went downhill fast, and died three weeks after my brother. Then, a couple of months later, two cousins in Indiana got into an altercation over a woman, and killed each other in the fight. There was another family death after that. We lost most of my Mother's side of the family that year; it was insane! Mom had had enough. It was more than one human being could take. She decided to head out West, to start a new life. We packed our bags, jumped in Grandma's green Cadillac, and drove. We didn't know where we were going, but, seeing the country west of the Mississippi on our drive, was an adventure that aided in soothing our broken spirits, and lightening our shattered hearts. There's something about an endless horizon and open land that pushes away pain. We took the southern route, which is part of the original route 66, westward. We stopped in Albuquerque, New Mexico on the way, and into old town, which I fell in love with! The Earth glistened out West. Every day, the sky was clear, bright and pale blue. Most often the only clouds were the com-trails from planes high, glowing sliver overhead, like a speck of dust caught in a stream of sunlight. I don't believe adobe structures are an acquired taste; they are made to mimic the surrounding landscape, rising from the ground and melting into the horizon. Can beauty or aesthetically pleasing describe a peaceful stirring of the soul?

We continued on, Mom deciding to stop in Phoenix, Arizona to visit her favorite Uncle Johnnie Jones. We all enjoyed the desert, and decided to rent a house a couple of blocks from Uncle Johnnie's house. We stayed in Arizona for a couple of years, but when an economic recession gripped the country, especially in the southwest, jobs dried up and we were forced to return to Chicago. As desperate as things were, I was unwilling to leave. To my bitter dismay, there were no options at that particular time, and I begrudgingly drove back East with Mom.

The last few years in Chicago had not been easy or kind to me, previous to Arizona. I had left school against my Mothers will. The gang situation had created issues walking to and from school through what was considered 'territories', one needed 'permission' to pass through a length of sidewalk. I was sorely disappointed in the educational system, and felt lost in redtape. In the job market, I had problems keeping positions; being lied to continuously by employers, saying the job was permanent, when they actually only needed to fill a spot until the person I replaced came back, from maternity leaves or vacations. It seemed every time I began to feel secure, I was suddenly seeking another position. I was always released for non-specified reasons. I couldn't get a break! Becoming tired of this one day, I confronted an employer who attempted to give me a pink slip. He, as all the others had said my work was superb and I am a delight but... This particular boss brought me into his office, pushing my last paycheck towards my hand. I refused to accept it. Instead, I sat down quietly and said, "If I am all these things, the customers like me, and I am creating profits for the business, it does not make sense that I would be released, fired. I demand you explain your actions!" My boss was then in the defensive position, stumbling over his words, and finally admitted, "I hired you until another employee returned from maternity leave." I said, "Then, you are pretty close to a scumbag, and you should have been honest with me. I would have accepted the position with the understanding that it wasn't permanent." I had my say, and felt proud of myself as I grabbed the check out of his hand and walked out of the office.

I had acquired a car back in Arizona, and it was having mechanical issues. I had it serviced and the next day, when I was leaving for another endless job interview, it wouldn't start! I went to open the hood of the car, and I couldn't get the latch to release, frustrating me more. I lost it, and began beating the car with my fists, kicking and screaming at it. Then, I stomped upstairs to phone the job site to tell them I couldn't make it in. They said I should not bother to show up anytime then. After hanging up the phone, feeling completely dejected, I heard a voice yelling my name from the street, saying my name over and over. Angrily, I stuck my head out of the window overlooking the street. It was an old acquaintance named, Jill, asking if I was okay. I was surprised, since the last time I had seen this person, I didn't like her, nor did she like me. Then she asked if I had a cup of coffee? Taken off guard, I said, "Yes", and told her to come up, we became fast friends after that. I had only one other real friend; back in New Jersey, my cousin, Robin. In between all of those years, I remained primarily alone with only a small scattering of people I considered friends. Jill and I became inseparable, and we supported one another through trying times.

One evening, Jill accompanied me on a job interview to the Red Apple lounge for a cocktail waitress position. As we sat and waited for the manager, a man came to the table and stood beside me. I remember looking to see only his legs, and had to sit back deep into the booth to take him all in. He was 6'7", what I call a 'tall drink of water'! He said that they had already chosen someone for the position. I was crushed. I wanted a drink, but we didn't have much money. The manager said that a wet tee-shirt contest was going on in the next room, and anyone that entered would get two free drinks. I didn't know what a wet tee-shirt contest was, but I agreed, and, signed on. After a couple of drinks, and a few more, sent our way from guy's waiting for the show, it was announced that the contest would begin in ten minutes; that was our cue to go back stage and get ready. There were a bunch of beautiful girls frantically prepping themselves. Then the festivities began. I followed the lead of the other girls, as I watched from backstage. There was a large plastic child's swimming pool set up on stage, from which a dude would take icy cold water to pour all over you, and then you did what you could to entertain the crowd, which was made up mostly of men, the room now filled to capacity. I think the mere fact of a woman with hard nipples poking tauntingly through the tee-shirts were more than enough for them!

My turn came, and I did my thing; a little dance and prance, making it up as I went along, borrowing from the best of what the other girls did, to wild applause and hoots! I was surprised! I am not built like a "brick house"; (Mom always called me, "the itty bitty titty committee".) Whatever I had done, it grabbed attention. I was in first place when, the contestant I was up against in the final round lifted up her shirt, breaking the rules by exposing herself, but instead of being disqualified, she took first place! I was runner up. We all had a good time, and the woman who had flashed everybody came to me backstage and gave me her card and said, I should consider becoming a model. She and a lot of the other girls were from her agency, plants to get other woman to enter the contest, and show the guy's a good time, and buy lots of drinks. I called the agency the next day, interviewed, and I was in. Cool! I had ended up with a job anyway.

The modeling job required a lot of traveling in the city and suburbs. I had a lot of fun and new adventures. Sometimes, men would approach me, looking for a date, sometimes waiting in the parking lot near my car. This made me very uncomfortable, and a bit scared. I enlisted Jill as my bodyguard, and when my rearview mirror fell off, she became that too. I was doing very well at this job, and made a handsome amount of money, which created some jealousy of other models in the agency. Eventually, I was told by my boss that some of the girls had gotten together and said they would leave if I didn't. Lost another job! It may sound strange, but I have never lost a position due to anything I had ever done or not done; it has always been because a female decided it was me or her, and I always lost!

Jill had lost her job at the same time at a box factory. We were both emotional messes, not being able to find new jobs. Each morning, for us, 3pm, we would call one another to meet for coffee at Bob's Egg Palace. Bob's was a greasy spoon diner open for breakfast and lunch only, we were the only persons left at the end of their day. They let us stay while the staff cleaned, and walked out the door as they locked up for the night. The restaurant was tucked between other shops in the middle of the block on the main drag of our neighborhood; Cermack street. I swear it's been there since the turn of the century, judging from the thick layers of grime and grease built-up over 20 coats of paint, peeling here and there. It still retained the original tin ceiling, though it was covered by a white, or should I say gray, coats of paint and grease and cigarette residue. I always expected to see a cockroach scooting out from somewhere, but despite its poor presentation of a cleanly establishment, I never did see anything that would indicate a serious health code violation. We were down to scraping up pennies to afford this luxury of dinning out. We helped one another through these most difficult times, but, sometimes it was not always enough.

Chapter Sixteen

Visit from an Angel

To say I was despondent would be a great understatement. I couldn't find a job, Mom was struggling to bring in enough money to cover expenses, and I felt guilty that I couldn't contribute. No matter what I tried, I failed miserably. Actually, failing was about the only thing I did quite well! I felt like a burden. I had no control over my circumstances, and spiraled deeper and deeper into a depression without end. Each night, I would go into the kitchen and choose a collection of knives, sit at my desk in my converted back porch bedroom, laid out the knives in a row in front of me, and prayed for the courage to end this whole crazy affair called life. But, how could I do that to my Mom? How could I leave her alone after Bruce left her, her Mom left her? I was conflicted and sad and unlucky.

After many, many nights conducting this ritual of choosing assorted knives, I convinced myself I wouldn't be missed, and that I would be doing Mom a favor, because she wouldn't have to support me.

I sat, having gathered my selection of knives, and cried, at the end of each day, alone in my room, emotionally and spiritually depleted. This night was different though. This was the night I would end my suffering, and everyone else's. I grabbed one of the knives, and prepared to thrust it though my heart. I tapped out a last cigarette from the pack, and it fell from my hand to the floor. Cursing, I reached down to pick it up. As I bobbed up again, in the midst of rising, a brilliant light appeared beside and in front of me. The room was illuminated by a golden white, brilliant light. I gawked, frozen in place, unable to move. The light had a human-like form and told me, "You create your own reality, and you can control the circumstances of this life, but you must understand you create your reality."

The angel said other things that I have never been able to verbalize, but, I understood in a place deep inside it counsel. Then it disappeared. I sat upright in my chair, knife in one hand, cigarette in the other, and tried to understand what just happened. It was so real and omnipotent; nothing like this had ever occurred before. I was left with, with such a gracious, peaceful feeling, as though everything would be okay. I dropped the knife, smoked the cigarette and went to bed. As sleep eluded me, I grappled with what I had been told, going back and forth internally on how hard I tried and struggled, while the world still seemed to undermine me, beyond my best efforts. Then I understood. It was my attitude, my feeling like a constant victim, which continued to create and attract the same situations over and over again. I was, in essence, a victim, but I also attracted similar circumstances that maintained and mirrored what I had begun to believe about myself; that I was a worthless, disposable human being.

The angel instructed me to ask for what I wanted. I thought I had, but, really it was out of focus. What I did was grouse over what I didn't have, what I kept losing, with only a vague idea of something specifically different. And, that is not the same as stating a desire. I had to learn to recognize the seemingly subtle differences. I began to get my ideas in order, and start to truly looking at the thoughts and intentions, what I focused and concentrated on, and what I felt was missing. "What is it that I would like in my life?" I asked myself. I wanted to be loved, and to understand the meaning of life, and of God. Yes, this is what I desired, these things... The answer to those prayers would take me years into a journey I could not have predicted, nor comprehend at the time!

My Mother, Yvonne, was a part of a wonderful group of friends that would meet after she finished her shift at Dmitry's, the restaurant she worked at. It was an eclectic assortment of individuals, which included a genius, a chef, a musician and the like. One evening, another friend joined in to drink coffee and kibitz the evening away. His name was Stanley; he was a professional psychic. He impressed everyone with his insights and predictions. Mother eventually scheduled a reading from Stanley. She was so blown away by his accuracy that, she thought I might get a handle on

things by consulting with him.
Mother knew I was not a happy camper, but, she had no idea how down and low I was.

I was not really interested in seeking this person's counsel, or anyone's counsel for that matter, but, I showed up for the appointment she made for me. Little did she or he know that I had desires of ending this affair called life, despite that angelic visitation, and information given to me. I intended to end it, no matter what this guy had to say!

I had become deeply skeptical of everything and everyone. I had decided that regardless of what this dude had to say, I was going to follow through with my plans, and remove myself from this plane of consciousness.

Dutifully, I went at my Mother's behest. I arrived at a wood framed two story apartment building. I went to the first floor apartment and knocked on the door. A man answered with a great smile and laugh, introducing himself as Stanley, and invited me in. Immediately, I put off by this person who could smile and laugh and be jovial. His flat had piles of newspapers stacked feet high, lining the entire length of an eight foot wall of the living room. It was definitely a bachelor's apartment, not terribly clean, items of clothing thrown here and there. He directed me to a couch, and cautiously I sat, wondering where this was going to go. Stanley continued to smile and laugh heartily aloud, which I hated more and more as the moments went by. He cordially offered me coffee, a good move, being a coffee-holic. I declined, and he began to drift closer to me as he "read" me. He said things like, "spirit says", and, "jou know, "I vould say to jou", he was a Polish national, naturalized; his accent was not too thick to understand. He did have a way about him that attempted to disarm, but, I wasn't going for it. "Ha!" I thought; "you don't know shit! You don't know I am going to commit suicide within forty eight hours, do you?" I mentally challenged. But, I think he did... He said during the reading that I had some choices to make, and that one of them regarded him 'seeing' me sitting on a street corner, waiting for a truck. He looked deeply into my eyes and without words, described what I was to do next. He told me that things would change for the better in two weeks. He said that I would be married, and I would grow more powerful in my abilities. He knew I was psychic. "Yeah, right! I couldn't even get a date! Shithead!" I thought. Yet, he was sorely accurate with other information he had related. I left there, still hating his laugh and smiles. The reading made me think, "what if he was right? What if I give it two weeks and see if his 'sight' bore any truth?" I thought about it. As lost and depressed as I was; still, to cause my Mother harm, if any opportunity allowed for me to spare her pain, there was no question that I would take it. I cried and howled bitterly at the delay!

Chapter Seventeen

A Troublesome Spirit

Jill and I continued to hang out and support one another. Our lives were going on different paths, though I was unaware of it at the time. Meeting at Bob's Egg Palace one afternoon, Jill mentioned she was having problems sleeping because, every time she closed her eyes, an undeniable presence, a cool, still brush of cold would come close to her face, and demand attention. The presence had become so persistent; she was becoming afraid to sleep in her own bed. Jill asked if I could come over and deal with the spirit, and ask it what it wanted, and tell it to go away. She lived on the ground level of a small mansion her parents owned. I, however, encouraged her to talk to it, since the spirit was trying to get her attention, not mine. She said she was too freaked out to attempt this. So I went over her house and did a walkthrough of the area. That entailed opening up my psychic senses, and slowly moving through the 'hot-spots' of the property. A hot-spot are areas where people sense, or observe energetic activity. Psychically, I found that rooms had been changed from the original layout. As I moved from room to room, I felt that there were doors that should have not been there. Walking through the door, I felt the sensation that the air or space was somehow condensed. I had the feeling/sensation of passing through a solid object; very weird! Where walls had been torn down, I could feel pressure. Where walls had been built, I felt I could pass right through. There was a moment when I came to a particular wall, very deeply into the psychic scanning work. I had my hands out in front of me as I walked, sensing the energies through the tips of my fingers, stretching out my senses... At that wall that had not existed in the past, I swept my right hand across it, and it went through the wall into the next room! Jill screamed, which knocked me out of this semi-trance, and I too realized what had just happened, as I withdrew my hand. Surprise cannot come close to what we had just witnessed. She asked me to do it again. I, too, wanted to, but it never did occur. I sensed through feeling, sight, smell. In certain rooms, sensations caused me to cough, as though a great amount of dust filled the area. Other areas had particular smells and temperature variations. This was my girlfriend's house, which I had visited on many occasions, so it was truly fascinating doing this psychic walkthrough, and discovering all over again a place I thought I had known very well.

I had intended to psychically scan the area for the ghost or spirit causing Jill so much grief, attempting to pinpoint the entryway, a spot where the spirit travels back and forth through, like a type of portal. As I had swept through the house, I felt we were being followed. Every time I tried to see who or what it was, it would disappear or hide. I decided to trick it, and pretended to go into another room, but whipped around, and finally caught a glimpse of what followed us; her ghost! He was tall and wore a dark, full length cloak and a large brimmed hat. His features were obscured, and the spirit was definitely a male. He was not pleased that I was able to trick him, and promptly whisked by us, leaving behind a cold breeze in a closed, windowless room. Jill's eyes became wide, and she turned even paler than her usually fair skin! (Jill's skin was so fair, when we were bored, we would study the visible veins on her legs like road maps branching off, trailing through her body)

Later, Jill checked with her Father about the changes I sensed had been made to the property. He said that walls were moved many years ago to make the space an apartment. The space was originally divided into chambers for servants in days gone by; and rooms to store fruits and vegetables through the long winter months. Also, there were special rooms to receive coal to heat the house, the exact rooms that had caused me to cough! Jill was able to obtain the original blueprint plans of the house, and found the information I sensed was accurate. That was the first time I became aware of another facet of abilities from the dynamics of being psychic.

Jill asked if I would rid her of this troublesome spirit, whom insisted on interrupting her sleep. She said it scared her too much to try and establish contact herself. I agreed, and showed up the afternoon we had scheduled, to directly contact the ghost or spirit in her house.

The difference between a 'ghost' and a 'spirit', as I have found is; a ghost is like a memory loop or Memorex tape as I call it. The ghost will appear around the same time, location and generally does not interact with the current environment. It is an image or emotional memory caught in the ethers of time. Where, a spirit is a form of a personality of a formerly living person still interacting with the environment. It is curious, and seemingly limited in its impact upon the physical world or conscious recognition, yet able to influence somewhat. Like making its presence consciously known, manipulating objects, such as doors.

Arriving at her flat, I knocked a few times on the outer door of her apartment, and then rapped on the windows, but she didn't answer. Eventually, I let myself in, and decided to wait for her after finding it empty. I waited and waited, but she failed to show up. Frustrated, I decided to leave. As I opened the first door leading to a small vestibule, and an entrance leading under the street, I glimpsed in the dark the large outline of a man, with fist up in the air, just readying to knock on the door. I was scared momentarily by this strange, shadowy figure on the other side of the door, but it was only Daniel, Jill's ex-husband, coming to check if everything was alright. He had seen me go into her apartment, but not leave. I said I was well, and told him I had an appointment with Jill, but I was tired of waiting. I invited him inside, and we sat and talked a while, waiting for her to return. I didn't know much about Dan, and we sat and enjoyed each other's company for a while. Finally, Jill arrived back home, we all had small conversation, and then he left.

I was somewhat annoyed; Jill was three sheets to the wind, having partied at the local bar. She still wanted me to make contact with the ghost, and though if she fortified herself, she wouldn't freak out. I said that that is not how it works, and considered whether I should proceed. Before I could come to a conclusion, Daniel returned, and we invited him in. We talked for a few hours and partied. He was in no condition to drive or even walk home, as he lived on the other side of town, so we asked him to stay. He wasn't too sure about that, but, a spark developed between us, and Jill was being very gracious, so he agreed.

Jill and Dan had had a difficult marriage, being married as teenagers, and a volatile break-up, but with me there, he felt as ease. As the summer night wore on, we noticed the room becoming colder and colder. Jill did not have air-conditioning so, that was strange. It got to the point where we all became uncomfortable and decided to turn in. Unfortunately, there was only one large bed, ok, this is different, I thought, but we were all friends, so we piled under the blankets and cuddled in a communal group hug. We were all quite tired, and simply cuddled together, me in the middle; Jill to my right, and Dan to my left. We all began to drift into sleep. Even though we were under a thick blanket, all cuddled together, the cold wouldn't go away. It seemed to get cooler and cooler until finally I got up, and grabbed a comforter from a cabinet, and threw it over the three of us. I squished in between the two as we all tried to warm up. Again relaxed, we all began to drift, edging sleep. Then, I became aware of a presence, one that seemed to creep closer and closer to me. My friends seemed to be sleeping, and I didn't want to disturb them. Whatever it was, it felt cold and menacing, and was not happy we were there! Then I sensed it right next to me, and angry! A slow cold swept across my body; every nerve seemed to tense. All of a sudden, all three of us bolt upright at the same time! They hadn't been asleep as I thought Jill and Dan both stated that they had been frozen with fright, and didn't dare move. We all looked around, not leaving the bed, then slipped under the covers, heads included, and tried to ride out the night. I told Jill I finally understood why she was so stressed, and that I was determined to help her out.

We all went to Bob's Egg Palace in the morning. None of us had really gotten much sleep. Daniel was hungover, and sat in a lump, slumped up against the wall of our booth. Jill and I went over the events of the evening. I asked her, "When did you first become aware of the presence?" Jill said, "I've sensed it on and off as long as I could remember, but, these last few months the ghost has gotten aggressive." I asked, "What do you mean?" Jill said, "The spirit harasses me, especially during bedtime. The lights would turn on and off at inopportune moments and then, I would find the bulb usually burned out the next day." His palpable presence just popping up, scaring her when she least expected, going about the regular routines of living. Jill wasn't inexperienced when it came to psychical activity; she was naturally intuitive. She had sensed presences before, her instincts well honed, but this one truly disturbed her and, felt the harassment was escalating. Daniel sat quietly listening to the conversation, not buying the idea she had a ghost. He started to tease her, trying to make a joke out of the situation. She was not amused! I interjected, stating to Daniel that the world is a strange place. He didn't have to believe necessarily in ghosts or spirits per se, but what we had all experienced last night could be explained or labeled that way. This seemed to make sense to him, thinking back a few hours ago, how cold the room became, the uncanny feeling of being watched and stared at, the inference of feeling threatened. It was definitely a new experience for him and he couldn't quite figure out what had actually occurred. I was intrigued he didn't simply dismiss our mutual experience, like most are prone to do. Jill said her parents were going out of town for the upcoming weekend, and asked if we could deal with the problem as soon as possible. I told her that would work. I wanted to find the portal the ghost was traveling through. I don't know why it seemed important, but I had begun to learn to listen to my instincts. We made a date, I reminded her to stay sober, and all went our separate ways.

It was a beautiful warm summer afternoon in the city as I made my way from my house two blocks away. Everyone in the neighborhood seemed to be out on their porches enjoying the weather and the weekend. Friends and families gathered on their small green patches of yard, their private sanctuaries. Smoke and the smell of lighter fluid, sausages and burgers from every yard laced the gentle breezes off Lake Michigan about four miles away. The people had beer and pop, as they call it in the mid-west, buried under ice in large coolers. Men closely tended flaming grills. Kids were running around. It was like a spontaneous festival had sprouted up and down the blocks. Summer in the city! I walked down the seven or so cement steps to Jill's basement flat and knocked on the door. No response. Then I tapped on the window, having momentary flashbacks of the last time we made this date. After she didn't appear, I tried the door, which I found unlocked and went inside to see if she was home. She was, buried under a pile of blankets and clothes, two super-sized Doberman Pincers on the bed, and her head on the wrong end of the bed. I dragged her ass out of bed, put on a pot of coffee, and waited for her to become conscious. Neither Jill nor I woke up well, and it was safest to not talk and leave us alone until the caffeine and nicotine jolted some energy into our brains. As she sat in her own private oblivion, I did another walk-through of the apartment, and also went upstairs to the main living quarters, to check it out. Jill said that the ghost moved throughout the property. She had on several occasions gone upstairs to her parents' apartment to sleep on a couch to get away from the spirit, but it simply followed her. Scanning the area, I finally found what I was looking for; the portal, cool! I wandered back downstairs and told Jill what I had found and suggested we begin on the main floor. She didn't need to do anything per se, but she was the focus of the 'haunting', so I sort of used her as bait. We went to the front of the upstairs apartment where she had two couches facing one another, and I called to the spirit to come out and join us. Jill sat semi-petrified, not sure what would happen. I tried to comfort her and said everything will be alright it, the ghost, couldn't really hurt her; most people hurt themselves when they are scared. She calmed a bit until the ghost showed up. She nearly crawled out of her skin, saying she would prefer to leave. I ignored her as I began asking questions, addressing the ghost directly. I asked, "Who are you?" He said, "My name is John." I asked, "What year is it?" He said, "It's 1883 and I own all of this land around here for eighty miles." I asked, "What are you doing here in this house?" He said, "I have enjoyed this house, it being so large and I moved in when it was built a few years before the turn of the century." He continued, "The house I built was much smaller, but it has all of the comforts one could buy." I asked, "Where is your family?" He said, "I never married, and I live here alone. I am a business man with landholdings, farming endeavors, which this property was located on, and gambling." He was pretty well to do, and very headstrong! The ghost would vary between being quite congenial to angered, and somewhat put off by these questions from a woman.

He said that this was his property, that his house had been demolished so, he was claiming Jill's house as his property, claiming it was his "birthright". I didn't understand what this meant, and attempted to explain that he was dead, and he needed to move on to a far, far better place. I mentioned he didn't seem very happy being here, and asked if he wouldn't prefer a more pleasant environment? He didn't seem to grasp the being dead part. It was as if I was speaking to him on a cell phone and whenever I referred to him as being dead, my voice would cut out. He simply wouldn't hear that he was existing on an alternative plane or dimension, and that he could choose to move to another one. At the time, I didn't know I could call a spirit guide or helper to the situation to assist the confused spirit. Essentially getting nowhere, the man refusing to leave, I asked if he would consider not scaring my friend. He was unaware that his antics were truly frightening and disruptive to her, and agreed. He wasn't malicious, but curious. He also found Jill very attractive and enjoyed marveling at her beauty.

I asked Jill if she could deal with this arrangement. She said it was fine with her, and demanded privacy in the bathroom! Everybody, as it were, was happy... My job was done.

After that intervention, Jill reported that the haunting and harassment was down to a low roar. She still sensed John about and actually, after witnessing our little confrontation with the spirit, wasn't as scared. If he bothered her, she would respectfully ask him to bug-off! Other members of the family did not have issue with John, and barely knew he was there. John still had fun every once in a while playing with peoples' heads, like moving items that had just been placed down; taking a spoon being used to stir a pot of soup, and hiding it in the laundry room, etc. But overall, life became a lot easier once contact had been established. Every now and again, I would connect up with John so see how it was going. He seemed a lot happier. I was curious about his feelings. John said that he recognized he was dead, but was still not willing to cross that boundary. However, he began to travel more and had met up with friends and family, and his sense of isolation disappeared. I noticed another spirit by his side. He winked at me with an energy about him that felt strangely familiar, not unlike that angel I encountered. The spirit was a sort of angel; he was a spirit-teacher assisting John, and befriending him until he was ready to make some changes. I was pleased for John, and felt a sense of accomplishment in assisting everyone involved all the way around.

Years later, John visited me at my marital home. He had come to say goodbye. I am laughing right now as I write this because the incident was so strange and amusing at the same time. I was sitting in my living room watching television, and reading a book. I sensed a presence by the front door, which I was facing. As I looked up from my book, I saw a giant man in a large brimmed black hat with a silver band, standing with his hands on his hips, except his hips were at floor level! I only had the top half of him! He smiled at me and sent his biddings of farewell and thanks. Then, after a few long minutes he slowly faded away. I was alone upstairs, Mom down in her little apartment studying; my husband out with the boys that night, and my daughter was sleeping. After John left, I went down to Mom's apartment to see how she was doing. She sat on her couch, somewhat glued in her seat, appearing pale. I was concerned and asked her, "What's the matter?" She said, "I had taken a break from studying to watch a program on television, when I sensed someone standing next to me. I looked over and seen boots with silver buckles and the legs of a giant man rising up through the ceiling!" I laughed and laughed. She had gotten John's bottom half! And it was in the exact spot where I had seen him upstairs. I explained the situation and she relaxed a bit, weirded out, but understanding. Funny, funny! A cup of Earle Grey tea soothed her jitters.

Afterward

It seems my youth was about discovering all the nuances of being aware of more than the physical world, that a plasticity existed. I was fortunate. To have chosen parents that didn't always believe what I was saying about my experiences, but, did not summarily dismiss it either. I think too, my parents had a hard time explaining away how I knew when someone would call, or was able to ask questions about the conversation from the other end of the phone line, that I was way too young to even understand! Father was good at simply filing these oddities away, and to not think about them. Mother was curious, and it expanded her ideas of what is possible.

I learned to control to a large extent, the influx of information, and the nature of that information. There was still a long way to go though, recognizing and understanding that being psychic is not unlike any innate skill or ability: Some of us are born mechanically inclined, some are great with numbers... These are natural talents or gifts that must be honed, explored and, to a degree, honored. I found out the hard way, as most lessons in my life, that to dishonor a gift by refusing it has its repercussions and consequences', and they are not all pretty!

In the next volume, we move from my youth into adulthood. The time of discovery and exploration is now evolved regarding that ‘plasticity’ of and about life.
I said prayers after the visitation from the angel that were about to fall into line, and become my reality for the next twelve years.

Appendix A

In The Beginning

This appendix is dedicated to my start in life, through my Mother's reminiscence of my youth. Our journey's in life are unique yet, we all share commonalities of a human experience.

The moment of birthing is the most difficult experience a woman manages to survive. The intense beauty of such intimacy; a single event beings' share is etched upon memory. My Mother's first birthing experience with my brother was arduous and scarring, both physically and emotionally. Before the doctor got to the delivery room, the baby's size began to tear and rip her; the baby was being pushed deeper and harder into life by natures' forces. The attending physician finally arrived, as the baby crowned, and delivered a strapping, healthy baby boy. That baby boy was pissed! He cried in anger as he was thrust into this world. It was cold at first, and the bright lights were not pleasant; healthy lungs challenged any complacency. Then, soft warm moist clothes caressed and cleansed, soothing this new life. Cries and screams mellowed into squeals, then coos, then sleep. She was stitched inside and out.

It's funny how a woman forgets the pains of labor once her child is upon breast, warm and snuggled close. Pain is forgotten to an extent, but not fear. No, fear has its residual effects, yet freakishly not dampening the desire or want, and sometimes need, to birth once more.

Mom's Reflections:

Two years after I gave birth to my son Bruce, I longed to have a daughter. I prayed, lit candles, made a novena, took my temperature, nothing. Always battling weight, I got down to a trim 120 pounds. It was nearly four years gone by attempting to become pregnant. One day I weighed myself and found I gained ten pounds. I went to my family doctor. He gave me an exam. The doctor had a look of concern and said he felt a tumor on my ovary and thought I might have cancer! He wrote out a prescription for a medication to shrink the tumor and eventually dissolve it. In the 1960's, the only thing labeled on a prescription bottle were directions for use, an expiration date and the patients name. I continued to gain weight and I continued to have internal exams to track the progress of the tumor. A close friend suggested I consult another physician, an OBGYN. I made an appointment with Doctor's Higdon, Bogard and Fox. As doctor Higdon was pulling off the examination gloves he smiled and said; "A lovely baby girl is on the way!" Of course he was teasing, knowing I already had a son. Concerned that I had taken the prescription for a tumor, the doctor said we would keep a close eye on the pregnancy. After much ado, I was finally pregnant! The excitement cooled as I remembered the delivery of my son. For months sleep was a stranger. When I closed my eyes at last, I would dream of a shiny mahogany coffin with a huge silver lock, and instantly my eyes would open. I was so frozen with fear; I could not even move my fingers to touch my husband for help. This occurred night after night. The only thing I craved was cold, crisp iceberg lettuce. Close to the time of the delivery, I went to a psychic, Mrs. Duka, who had predicted the pregnancy a year prior. She assured me that the delivery would not be a painful experience like it was with the first child. Then she began to laugh. She said I was having a baby girl, and would be a handful, and that I would become pregnant soon after the delivery, which I did with my daughter Karen. I indeed had an easy labor and nearly painless delivery, awake all the while.

Soon after bringing my treasure home, there was again no sleep to be had, for the whole household was kept awake as Katie wailed and wailed! Sleep only came for this pink, miniature person, with fine black wispy hair, covering every inch of her body; pressed upon the warmth on my chest or her fathers'. My first child, Brucie did not cry like Kate did, she seemed to be in pain. After a few weeks, I became concerned she might be ill. Finally I called the doctor and learned she had colic. Medication took care of that.

As she grew, she was very attached to me, her dad and

brother, but no other family member or our friends could hold her. Once we put her in a crib from the bassinette, she started to rock herself to sleep. As she got older, the rocking increased, her dad found himself tightening the screws to the crib more often, and she eventually went through three cribs! She rocked on the couch, on the floor, against the wall, against a gate or fish tank and in the car. She even rocked when I held her. Folks thought that was so cute! After three years, I sought help. The doctor said Kate would most likely stop by the age of five, nope. She rocked in kindergarten and on and on. It was eventually suggested that Kate receive testing at Hackensack hospital. For three months she underwent mental and emotional evaluations. I was interviewed about topics concerning her home life and the pregnancy. Finally, when all the results came in, seven doctors and I sat in a conference room. The results: "An extremely intelligent child, physically normal. However, due to the anxiety during pregnancy, the child is highly insecure." They suggested a more relaxed school setting, and after much searching, I enrolled Kate in a special education program. She excelled academically in the first year, and went on to a regular school a few years afterwards. One day as Kate's dad was driving her to school he said to her, "Why can't you stop rocking?" She replied, "Why can't you stop smoking?" He was amazed that this child realized compulsion!

I also noticed, as Katie began to talk, that she would run to the phone before it rang and tell me who was calling, and what they would say. This opened my eyes that she had a special gift, which ultimately led me to explore areas of the paranormal.

We had moved to a new house and not too long after settling in, she would knock on my bedroom door and say, "Mom, someone is in the hallway but not!" This was at three in the morning, night after night. My son also had experiences with sensing a presence, noisy yet unseen.

Around the same time we had a dog named Scottie. He died and we buried him in the spot he like to lay back yard under some bushes. Often when Kate was playing outside, those bushes would jostle around, as if a wind picked up; but the leaves nor the bush itself, never moved. She would come inside and announce, "Scotties here!"

So many of the 'happenings' were so subtle that perhaps someone else may have overlooked or ignored them. I began to take Kate's experiences more seriously. She is aware of something few will acknowledge. There is more to life than sight can reveal, if we allow our other senses to emerge as she does automatically.

Kate would also recall things that happened before she was born. When she was old enough to draw freehand, she would labor for hours drawing picture after picture of schooners with five masts, from different angles. I didn't think about it at first, but eventually asked myself how she could draw such a complicated ship in such detail? So, I asked her why she keeps drawing the same ship over and over? She replied, “I don’t want to forget!” “Forget? Forget what?” I asked. “The ship I drowned on” came her matter of fact reply!

Appendix B

Below is a poem I wrote about the nature of energy, as I have experienced and understand it. Everything seems to have a 'consciousness', an aspect of a life force.

April 13, 1996 1:51pm Saturday Chgo. R.P.
Totd (thoughts of the day)

A mist rose gentle hugging hills and dales of lament
Vapors clung giving rise only to ridges piquing
It was those very ridges, reminding
Remaining, perhaps grounding my station

I walked upon this plane poised inside its static
Peering out and at juts distinguished
Its design portrayed the event of this horizon

And a wind grew from the east
The mist coagulated into deep clouds vibrating
The movement of the lands scape thickened
And collections of natures climbed into this mass
Now gaining strength
Graduating

Its propensity became a single vision of its many potentials
Focusing intently

The elements of time
The perimeters of environ
Shaped and then wielded a polarity
And begot a force
And this entity explored circumstance and influence within this
Place
Discovering through its very expression the essence of itself

Rising, falling, circulating throughout its realm
Experiencing power
Yet still untouched

A harbinger of energy filled presence
Creating definition
The expanse of awareness broadened
Reaching a boundary

The boundaries multiplied as observation increased
Intensified by curiosity
Now referred to a catalyst receptive
And the winds blew
Slowed by the trance induced by presence
(a minute significance)
refined
referenced a still small point

balancing
that of myself unfolding upon itself as a mist coalescing into a cloud

or
paused upon a precipice observing
becoming the experience
merging
into a dynamic absorbing reflection
into a vastness contained
within
yet realizing all the while I am the sum total
the paradoxical paradigmatic intent
enfolded

K.A. Ellis, Excerpted from, “Please be mine, Valentine”. (pub. 1997)

Additional Books By Kate Ellis

Word Search Puzzle Series:

Words *that* Empower Series:
Vol IX "Contemplations: (pub 2017)
Vol. VIII "Honor, Value & Integrity" (pub 2012)
Vol. VII "Your Callings" (pub. 2011)
Vol. VI "Enough-ism, blaze a unique trail" (pub. 2011)
Vol. V "Sayings of the Buddah" (pub. 2010)
Vol. IV "Graces" (pub. 2009)
Vol. III "On Prosperity and Wealth" (pub. 2007)
Vol. II "Essentials" (pub 1998/2008)
Vol I "The Word" (pub1997 out of print)

Non Fiction:

Did You Know... A message of Choice & Change (pub. 2006)
Worrier To Warrior, Conquer Anxiety & Panic Attacks (pub 2014)

Poetry:

Please Be Mine, Valentine (pub. 1997)
April Fools For Love (pub. 1996)
Soul in Chemical Clothing (pub. 1993)

Excerpt from Words that Empower Vol. III
By Kate Ellis,CCHt.

POWER

Q B B Y L R E W O P F O T N I O P P T I
T H E P O I N T O F I I B K P X O N S T
Q Z Q B W T N E S E R P E H T W I A P W
O T P Y G Z P P O A W O N Z E O L Y O A
Y F T H B Z A J Z G L J T R P W G T I W
O M P I D Y E X H J F H I R A K A O N E
U A P O Z G M C U X O S U Y A I I Z T V
R J P O W C O W S F T O S P Q L C K O M
P K N N W E P N X N Y I M F M Z N T F T
O J L O F E R U I S N Q L Q O K C N P N
W V T M M U R O I T U Y J T J N S I O E
E P D D Y M P I H A Y S V M L B I O W S
R S A Y E E A E S I L L P A L T T P E E
I N F D H Z P O G A S W W T S N N T R R
X N H T R R C D X J L A A Z X F E N F P
Z M X E E P G W J Z B W L Y B E S E W E
B C W S N K G L I C B V A W S T E S X H
N O E S G T I I Z K Q Y D Y A Z R E U T
P N O N B W Q Z I R K N D Y S Y P R J S
T T H E P R E S E N T U W I S W S P G I

THE POINT
POINT OF POWER
POWER IS
POWER IS ALWAYS
IS ALWAYS IN THE
PRESENT

THE PRESENT
PRESENT IS
IS ALWAYS
THE POINT OF
OF POWER
POWER

YOUR POWER
IS THE PRESENT
THE PRESENT
IS YOUR POINT
POINT OF POWER
PRESENT POINT

About Author

Kate Ellis,ccht is a Clinical Counseling Hypnotherapist in private practice for 30 years specializing in the relief & remission of anxiety and panic attacks. Kate is a consultant and teacher exploring psychological growth, the healing arts, intuition, creativity, hypnosis and spirituality and all the 'ologies' out there (sciences).

Kate proudly served as Vice President (2013-2015) and then President (2016—2017) for the Arizona Society for Professional Hypnosis. Founded in 1978 ASPH is Arizona's only independent professional hypnosis and hypnotherapy organization. It is one of the largest active groups in the country.

"My focus is my clinical practice however continue to provide clairvoyant medium readings/consultations & investigations. It's not something you can turn off, and suppressing these talents and gifts is not recommended. It has aided me greatly in my practice being able to intuit who is ready to be successful as well as 'inside' information. My clients are often unaware of my 'other' abilities and I like to keep it that way more often than not." Kate

www.ingramcontent.com/pod-product-compliance
Lightning Source LLC
La Vergne TN
LVHW090607110826
845146LV00001B/297

* 9 7 8 1 4 2 7 6 4 1 8 1 6 *